From SI

African Americans Come to Aurora, Illinois
1850 – 1920

Dennis Buck

From Slavery to Glory:
African Americans Come to Aurora, Illinois, 1850-1920

©2005 Dennis Buck

ISBN 0-9770896-0-6

First Edition, First Printing:
Aurora Historical Society
P.O. Box 905
Aurora, IL 60507-0905
USA

Front cover art: Photo of Carrie Jackson, taken by William Wilson c. 1913. The photograph, titled *"Aunty" Jackson's Reverie* is from the collection of the Aurora Historical Society.

Book printed in the United States of America by
River Street Press, Aurora, Illinois

Table of Contents

List of Tables	4
List of Maps	5
List of Illustrations	6
Introduction	8
Chapter 1: Dawn of a City	17
Chapter 2: Strangers Among Strangers	30
Chapter 3: Liberal Ideals, Racial Biases	64
Chapter 4: Unpleasant Glory	90
Afterward	137
Appendix: African American Census Data	
1850	140
1860	140
1870	141
1880	147
1900	155
1910	164
1920	174
End Notes	194
Sources Consulted	199
Index	206

List of Tables

Table 1:	Total Population of Aurora by Decade	29
Table 2:	Aurora's African American Population by Decade	41
Table 3:	Aurora's African American Population by Place of Birth	44

List of Maps

Plat of Aurora, 1836	21
1860 Map of the City of Aurora	23
1868 Map of the City of Aurora	39
1892 Map of the City of Aurora	52

List of Illustrations

Artist's view of the Fox River before settlement	16
Photograph portrait of Samuel McCarty	18
Photograph portrait of Theodore Lake	19
View looking west across Stolp Island	37
View looking north on Broadway	47
"Aunty" Jackson's Reverie	50
Group portrait of the Turkey Club	54
Photograph of F. T. Woolson's Barber Shop, 69 N. Broadway	55
Photograph taken inside an unknown saloon	58
View of the East Side showing three historic churches	66
Portrait of the Wagner family, by Sheldon Peck	69
Class portrait taken at New York Street School	86
Photograph of "Dubrock's Quartet"	88
Advertisement for Brown's Coal	89
Group portrait of "Pug's" Colts	91
Ben and Susan Carter Family	95
Photograph Portrait of Isaiah Carter	100
Mose Webb's Confectionary	103
Main Street Baptist Church	105
The "Barracks"	113
Unknown Home on New York Street	114
Class portrait taken at Brady School	116
Members of the Idle Hour Club making New Year's calls	119
Calathumpian Parade, 1913	122
West High students in blackface for a minstrel show	124
Henry Boger	127
Calvin Boger	128
Labor Day, 1903	134

To my Mom and Dad, whose fascination with language and history inspired my career, and whose compassion and love shaped my life.

Introduction

In the introduction to their history of Kane County, R. Waite Joslyn and Frank W. Joslyn explain the vitality and necessity of historical study.

> *[T]he history of a State, Nation, City or County, is but a composite biography of those who there worked, and by their efforts left to us who here follow them a hundred forces and tendencies that aid or retard our advancement. They left public opinions, social notions, business methods, forms of government, standards of morality, etc., etc., by which we are now controlled; and which are changed with difficulty.*[1]

In many respects, the collections of the Aurora Historical Society are a "composite biography" of the City of Aurora. The Historical Society was chartered in 1906 by a group of citizens who were distressed by the gradual disappearance of their heritage. This group's stated goal was to preserve the memory and the physical evidence of Aurora's founders and early citizens; those pioneers from the northeastern United States whose "efforts left us a hundred forces that aid or retard our advancement." Gradually, during one hundred years of continuous collecting, the makeup of the Historical Society's membership changed, and the artifactual and archival holdings that were gathered began to represent some of Aurora's ethnic diversity.

Regrettably, other gaps in the biography were not addressed. The Historical Society's holdings, and therefore its past exhibits and publications, contain little to represent the racial diversity that characterized most of the city's history. In particular, the glaring omission of African Americans from the early historical record is a serious problem.

A study of this topic was clearly long overdue. African Americans have had great formative influences on Aurora. Almost from its founding in 1834, the city was a hotbed of radical abolitionist activities. With the Protestant churches leading the way, Aurora became a vital stop on the Underground Railroad. While the number of people actively helping slaves to freedom through this secretive organization was necessarily small, evidence suggests that many Aurorans supported the work, or at the least did not hinder it. The 1860 Federal Census records a dozen free Black men, women and children in Aurora. The 1870 Census lists over 150 African Americans living and working in Aurora. Yet in spite of the fact that African Americans have been transforming the town socially and politically, and contributing to the City's development for over a century, there have been no formal studies of this population. Some historical projects have been and continue to be done in Aurora that relate aspects of this neglected topic. The local churches have produced anniversary histories, some individuals and families have done genealogical research, and the African American History Museum and Black Veterans Archive promotes awareness of the currents of history on a national level. My research tries to incorporate some of this information with official records, City Directories, newspaper articles and oral interviews and synthesize them into a cohesive story about the beginnings of African American settlement in Aurora.

A composite biography requires a background, what Joslyn and Joslyn termed the "recognized ways of doing and thinking."[2] Thus, Chapter 1 is an introduction to the civic history of Aurora. Understanding the history of the town prior to African American in-migration is vital, as that provides the context for the events that followed. These pre-existing patterns of life were an important force in shaping the outcome.

The next step is to introduce the main subjects. Using data compiled from the Federal Census reports and City Directories, the second chapter will look at the migration and settlement patterns of African Americans in Aurora between 1850 and 1920, with an emphasis on discovering when specific neighborhoods developed, where they were located, and what factors influenced the settlement patterns. When available, I will also try to interpret data on homeownership, education and employment, in order to identify key benchmarks of community growth and acculturation.

The third chapter will examine why African Americans generally, and slavery particularly, were subjects that obsessed Aurora's social, religious and political establishment in the middle of the nineteenth century. Organizations that were created during this period were manifestations of the "public opinions, social notions, business methods, forms of government [and] standards of morality" that were the legacy of the city. Many of the standards of belief and behavior that influenced the reception that African Americans experienced as new arrivals were molded through the actions and rhetoric of these groups.

The fourth chapter will address the reactions of white Aurorans to in-migration and settlement by African Americans, and compare those when possible with the response of African Americans to the dominant culture and the various sub-cultures of Aurora. Did the white residents of Aurora welcome Black men and women who settled in Aurora? How did African Americans view themselves in the context of the larger population? Did African Americans attempt to shoulder into the mainstream of local society and politics, or did they quickly form separate institutions? Through this process of comparison, we will also examine some of the culture and characteristics of the African American community locally.

Much of the data for this study was drawn from the Federal Census reports of 1850–1880 and 1900–1920 (Most of the 1890 Federal Census was destroyed in a fire). I have reproduced the entries for African Americans living in Aurora, by decade, in the Appendix at the back of this book. I believe that this will prove a useful tool for future research, and hope that I have managed to keep errors of transcription to a minimum. There are certainly errors in the original sources. The information contained in the censuses is an invaluable resource in historical studies such as this, but as anyone who has worked with them can attest, the records contained in these reports are only as accurate as the enumerators who amassed them. Missed households, strange entries, illegible handwriting and misinformation are familiar obstacles. Additionally, early census forms were not designed to accomplish much more than a basic counting. For the first few decades of this study, the addresses of the respondents were not recorded.

Fortunately, the political and business leaders of Aurora arranged for the publication of City Directories that incorporated data that the censuses did not, including addresses. Updated directories were printed at least every three years. Comparisons between the decennial census reports and the City Directories proved fruitful in fleshing out some of the details of African American settlement. However, there were also conflicts in the data. The addresses given in the directory do not always correspond with the wards listed in the census. Names in one source sometimes are not found in the other. In such cases of discrepancy, when it was impossible to determine which source was correct, this study favored the directory as more reliable, since it was produced locally for the convenience of Aurora's citizens.

Another difficulty encountered in this study was a lack of available resources from the African American point of view. Many of the men and women who migrated to Aurora in the nineteenth century were not literate and those who were rarely had either the time or the inclination to keep diaries or record their personal histories. No letters, written or received locally, are know to exist that discuss local politics, schools, business or social life from an African American perspective. Likewise, several of the oldest and most important local institutions were unable to add much to the historical record. St. John's African Methodist Episcopal Church and Main Street Baptist Church are the two oldest Black congregations in town. Both know their history and traditions. Both have a strong sense of their importance to the African American community and the city generally. Yet both lack records and photographs documenting the rich stories of their early history. Contemporary stories and announcements that appeared in the local press give some important insight into the dominant culture's perception of African Americans generally, and the local Black population to a lesser degree. But even that historical record grows hazy around the turn of the century. Accounts involving African Americans in Aurora virtually cease just before that portion of Aurora's population experienced its greatest growth.

In 1925, the Beacon-News initiated a weekly feature called *Now and Then*. The premise was to have Lewis "Lutz" White, a man steeped in local lore, relate stories and reminiscences of the "good old days." He also encouraged old-timers to write in and share their stories. The column was hugely popular and continued under White until 1935. Charles Pierce Burton took over the column from 1935–47, and Stanley Faye was the Historical Editor from 1947–48. The idea was picked up again by Robert Barclay in 1962 and carried on until 1976. These men helped to preserve hundreds of valuable stories that give the modern reader a peek into Aurora's past, and all local historians are in their debt. As wonderful as this historical resource is, however, it must be noted that almost all of these stories are told from the perspective of the White middle-class. Some of the stories allow glimpses of early African American settlers, but since they can not be fully corroborated they must be read carefully. With this admonition in mind, these stories can at least reveal some of the mindset of the culture group that produced them.

An entirely different set of concerns rises from the nature and purpose of the stories. When reminiscing about childhood, events take on a rosy glow. In addition, these memories were recorded with the knowledge that they were to be published in the paper. Stories of racial tension or strife would not be likely candidates, and if they were submitted they had to pass the editorial staff. In the end, what remains important is that these recollections provide some glimpses into Aurora's schools from the perspective of former students, into back alleys and shops, and other places that were seldom recorded by more traditional historical means.

The title of this book, From Slavery to Glory, is a phrase borrowed from an article that appeared in the Beacon in 1867. In that article the author, "Andy Lee, A C of A D" [which stood for "American citizen of African descent"], sketches his rise from bondage to participating member of the democracy. With historical hindsight, we know that the equality that Andy Lee called glory was not achieved in 1863 with the Emancipation Proclamation. It was not achieved in 1920, the endpoint for this historical account. After more than a century of struggle, prickly questions of prejudice and inequality remain. So where is the glory?

Think of the phrase "from slavery to glory" as a path that we walk together, Black and White. This study concludes in 1920 with the United States at a crucial crossroads of that path. The NAACP and the Urban League were reshaping the national political landscape while jazz and the Harlem Renaissance were beginning to push Black culture into the international spotlight. Locally, Aurora's growing African American population was also striving for recognition. Having marked some of the highlights of the first part of the path, it seemed appropriate to pause at a historical moment of such promise and change. Hopefully this book, like a pin in a map, shows where we have been and how much more ground we have to cover.

Producing this history has often been difficult, occasionally even intimidating. The original intention was to break new ground in an area of local historical study that had been neglected. When it became apparent that this study would be the first of its kind on the subject, the project took on new importance. The author hopes that this effort to uncover some of the early history of the African American community in

Aurora may spark further interest in the subject. Perhaps it may even pave the way for future discoveries of photographs, documents and three-dimensional artifacts, currently unknown and unavailable to researchers interested in pursuing this rich and important aspect of Aurora's history.

    No project of this scope is done alone, and I would like to thank the people without whom this book could not have been made: Langdon G. Wright, my advisor, teacher and friend, whose inexhaustible knowledge of history challenged me to find a deeper understanding of the national context of local events, and who helped me to piece a tangle of note cards into a cohesive narrative; the Board of the Aurora Historical Society, which allowed me to blend my Masters project into my work in 1998, and encouraged my efforts to publish my thesis for a wider audience; AHS Executive Director John Jaros, who has an encyclopedic awareness of Aurora's history and was an invaluable aid in identifying photos, locating sources and verifying dates; Dan and Dorothea Buck, Heather Buck, Erin Howard and Jennifer Putzier, all of whom proofed the text at various stages and provided countless ideas to improve both grammar and content; and Andy Buck, who edited the final text, pruning away unnecessary clutter and adding crucial, fresh insight when I could no longer distinguish good from bad. Special thanks go to my wife, Heather, whose patience and tolerance were sorely tested in 1998 with months of late nights spent in research and writing followed by the panicked frenzy of my thesis deadline, and now another year of much the same. I couldn't have done this without your love and support.

Unknown artist's depiction of the Fox River before the settlement of McCarty Mills in 1834. The large island in the channel is called Stolp Island because Frederick Stolp purchased the land from the U.S. Government in 1842 for $12.72.

From the collections of the Aurora Historical Society

-Chapter One-
The Dawn of a City

Aurora, Illinois is a blue-collar town in Kane County, forty miles west of Chicago. The buzz and hum of industry has been Aurora's theme from its founding in 1834. The men credited with founding the town, Samuel and Joseph McCarty, were not farmers coming west to plough and plant the rich prairie soil, but millers. They and the settlers who came after them built on a foundation of enterprise and trade, which gradually shifted to include manufacturing interests, local and national transportation networks and heavy industry.

The McCartys came to Illinois with a purpose. Acting on accounts of the water privileges being given out in the West by the federal government, first Joseph, and later Samuel left their home near Elmira, New York.[3] On a stretch of land along the Fox River they spied the perfect combination of natural resources necessary to their craft. The river itself was the prominent feature, with sufficient drop to power mill wheels and enough volume to navigate between the settlements that were springing up along its banks. Additionally, a number of sizable islands narrowed the channel, simplifying the task of dam building. Stretching north along the banks was an enormous stand of timber to be sawn into lumber for buildings. And farmers, enticed into the fertile Fox River Valley, would provide steady work for the grindstones. Joseph McCarty laid claim to 360 acres on the east side of the river, with a further 100 acres on the west bank, to ensure their rights to the water power.[4]

A strikingly similar set of circumstances gave rise to a separate development on the western bank of the Fox. A few months after Joseph McCarty staked his claim, Zaphna Lake arrived in the valley. He and his

Samuel McCarty, c. 1850. Although his brother Joseph arrived first, Samuel is generally credited with being the founder of Aurora. Samuel's political skills and instincts as a developer put Joseph's mill site on the path to becoming an industrial center and a destination for immigrants.

From the collections of the Aurora Historical Society

In addition to building a mill, Theodore Lake started the first store in Aurora and farmed. Like Samuel McCarty, Lake saw benefit in public improvements as well. He contributed regularly to build churches, though he was not a religious man, and pledged the considerable sum of $500 toward the building of the first bridge across the Fox.

From the collections of the Aurora Historical Society

brother, Theodore, had listened to the stories circulating about the bounty and promise of Illinois. They determined to investigate for themselves. Zaphna left Ohio on a scouting trip, with the understanding that, should rumor prove reality, he would buy land for them both. Impressed by the possibilities of the location, Lake purchased the land held by the McCartys on the west side of the Fox River. And, like the McCartys, he too established himself by first building mills.

From their founding, McCarty Mills (the East Side) and Hartford (the West Side) grew in parallel tracks. In the winter of 1835–36, the McCartys put their vision for a town on paper in the first plat. The following spring, Samuel McCarty improved the natural resources of the area by arranging to have the main east-west road in the region, which carried the stagecoach from Chicago to Galena, diverted through town.[5] The stage carried the mail, so within a few months planning was underway to build a post office. Part of that process involved choosing an official name for the town. After some debate, Aurora was selected.[6] By 1845, Aurora was a bustling village of one hundred souls, with farmers, merchants, mechanics, a tavern and a post office, in addition to the mills that gave her birth. On March 6, 1845, by vote of the residents, the village of Aurora was incorporated.[7]

Across the river, growth and change were occurring, though at a slower pace. Like her bustling neighbor, Hartford took economic advantage of the rich agricultural land of the surrounding area, not by farming, but with an assortment of merchants and businesses supplying the needs of farmers, and grist mills and woolen mills to process what the farmers produced. Theodore Lake laid out a town plat in 1842, and assigned it the name West Aurora.[8] However, unlike their neighbors, the

Plat Book of Aurora, Kane County, Illinois (being copies of the plats as recorded for record in the recorder's office of Kane County, Illinois). Rockford, IL: The Thrift Press.

From the collections of the Aurora Historical Society

West-Siders were in no hurry to alter their status. The vote to incorporate West Aurora failed utterly on two separate occasions, and the village was not finally incorporated until 1854.[9]

Ironically, while Aurora and West Aurora grew in similar directions during this twenty-year prelude, they simultaneously fell into sharp competition with each other. Naturally, competition arose over economic concerns related to building two mill towns in such proximity—literally a stone's throw from each other across the river. Aggravating the situation was the Fox River itself. Bridges built across the river regularly washed away. Until 1845, the only reliable means of crossing from side to side was a ferry.[10] The river was a very real physical barrier, and a psychological hurdle that prompted the development of distinct cultural differences.

In spite of the tensions, in 1857, by vote of the citizens and by action of the Illinois Legislature, the two towns bound themselves together as the City of Aurora.[11] Obviously nervous about the likelihood of success for the merger, the leading citizens and the legislators employed four rather unusual methods to overcome the legacy of competing interests and political jealousy. To calm fears that one side would take political control and dominate the other, the city charter required that elections for mayor be held every year. Furthermore, all four of the city's wards were laid out spanning the river, like stitches closing a gaping hole. As additional assurance of neutrality, the charter specified that city hall and the other municipal buildings be built neither on the east nor the west side of the river, but on the large island known as Stolp's Island. Finally, there seems to have been some form of

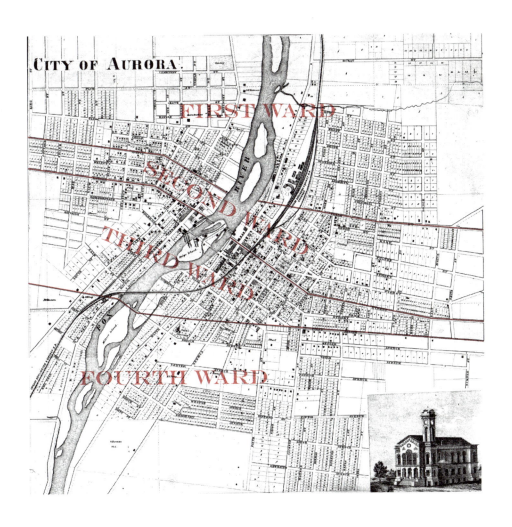

Map of Kane County, Illinois, From Original and Recent Surveys By, and Under the Direction of Adin Mann, County Surveyor. Philadelphia: Matthews, Crane & Co., 1860.

From the collections of the Aurora Historical Society

"gentlemen's agreement" that the office of mayor would alternate each term, with the first mayor coming from the West Side, the next from the East, and so on.[12]

While they continued to clash like jealous siblings, businessmen on both sides of the river recognized that transportation was beneficial to everyone. Samuel McCarty's successful bid to re-route the road from Chicago to Galena in 1836 had connected them to other towns where they could market goods and produce. Most significantly, the road linked them to Chicago, a large ready market and a connection to the railroads moving east. The new road also brought scores of people through the fledgling towns; people searching for a propitious location to settle and realize their dreams of carving out their fortunes in the West. Aurora continued to grow and thrive as an important center of local trade. The population raced past twelve hundred in 1850, just sixteen years after its founding.[13] Also in 1850 the Federal Census recorded, for the first time, African American residents in the City of Aurora.

The rural village atmosphere began to change in 1849, when several men in Aurora created a small branch railroad. This road, through growth and mergers, developed into the Chicago, Burlington and Quincy Railroad (C. B. & Q.), one of the largest and most important arteries of the West. Having such an enterprise in town was a critical step in Aurora's history for three main reasons. The first and most obvious result was direct employment. In 1856, the C. B. & Q. elected to locate its shops in Aurora. The shops, where engines and cars for the entire line were manufactured and repaired, instantly became the primary employer in town, and remained so for decades. Equally important was the railroad's role as a catalyst for growth. A major rail line centered in town encouraged other large businesses and manufacturers to move in. Finally, the railroad was a fast transportation link to Chicago, already the rail hub of the nation. The trains carried waves of new people who were looking for work in the increasingly industrial and urban community on the prairie.

Aurora followed a path similar to Chicago, her mammoth neighbor to the east. The rail lines that connected the two cities benefited Aurora economically. However, she was not overwhelmed and absorbed by Chicago. Partly, this was due to distance, Aurora being around forty miles to the west. More importantly, Aurora developed and maintained a distinct identity. The addition of fast and reliable transportation to the existing mix of industry and trade made Aurora a logical place for new industries to locate. A diverse range of business and manufacturing, from casting and assembling iron cooking stoves to sewing ladies underwear, settled into the area to take advantage of the vast markets made possible by the C. B. & Q. Each new venture meant jobs. Immigrants from Sweden, Germany, Ireland, Romania and Luxembourg, as well as migrants from states in the South and East, followed the siren call of economic opportunity to Aurora. By 1870, this included a growing enclave of African Americans.

Thus, like other industrial centers in the United States, Aurora grew to a city of some size, with a population of people from a variety of cultural backgrounds, assembled through the upward spiral of prosperity. By 1890, the population of Aurora had soared to almost 20,000. In the following decade the population continued to balloon, expanding at around twenty percent annually.[14]

Ethnic and racial diversity was not truly a reality in Aurora until the coming of the railroad. The opening of the C. B. & Q. shops in 1856 brought thousands of people in search of work. Susan Palmer, in her study of Mexican and Romanian immigrant communities in Aurora, notes that "Aurora really lost its frontier homogeneity and village ambiance during this time as the population leapt from twelve hundred to nearly twelve thousand."[15]

The decision to locate the railroad shops, the city's largest employer, in the northeastern quarter of the city made a lasting impression on Aurora's physical and cultural geography. The majority of the newcomers settled on the east side of the river to be near their work, whether in the railroad shops or one of the new industries that had been lured into Aurora in the wake of the C. B. & Q. As a result, the residents of the East Side, with the exception of one neighborhood in the southeast, were primarily working and middle-class, and increasing numbers of them were recent immigrants.[16]

Meanwhile, the West Side gradually gained a reputation for being the home of Aurora's elite. People around town began referring to the Downer Addition, then the western edge of town, as "Quality Hill" because a number of Aurora's wealthy entrepreneurs and businessmen built beautiful and expensive residences there.[17]

Of course, it would be a gross oversimplification to say that the river acted as a fence separating the wealthy business owners from their workers. Not all of the manufacturing and enterprise was on the East Side. Rathbone, Sard and Company Stove Works, Aurora Brewing Company, Hercules Iron Works and other industrial firms elected to locate in the western half of the city. There were also hotels, stores, banks and shops on the West Side. The working-class and middle-class employees who staffed these places lived near their work and brought class, race and ethnic diversity into neighborhoods west of the river. Moreover, many politically powerful and wealthy families lived on the East Side. Without question, though, the bulk of Aurora's population lived east of the river, and as the city's population boomed in the decades around the turn of the century the East Side neighborhoods contained a broader mixture of European immigrants and transplanted workers from around the country.

Migration is traumatic. Tearing oneself away from one's home and relocating to an area where new and strange customs and conduct prevail is difficult, even when the decision to do so is made willingly and eagerly. Thus, whether they travel overseas or from city to city, immigrants seek out people like themselves. In both urban and rural settings, people of common heritage and background generally choose to live, work, worship and recreate as a group. This is, of course, also true of members of the core culture, although seldom are the members of the dominant group that self-aware. As Milton Gordon pointed out in his study of immigration in the United States, "the white Protestant American is rarely conscious of the fact that he inhabits a group at all. *He* inhabits America. The *others* live in groups."[18] [Emphasis his]

Between 1850 and 1870, a progression of culturally directed institutions ascended to prominence in Aurora. In 1851, Sacred Heart became the city's first Catholic parish. When that first church building burned in 1868, the predominantly Irish congregation elected to rebuild on the East Side, where most of them lived. By then, there were two new Catholic parishes on the East Side, one conducting services in

German and the other in French. There were also Protestant churches conducting services in German and Swedish.[19] By 1868, the German population in Aurora grew large enough to support a German-language newspaper, the <u>Volksfreund</u>.[20] Around the same time, the rival <u>Beacon</u> advertised aggressively their "complete assortment of German face metal and wood type, for the execution of all kinds of German cards, circular, and poster printing."[21] The Germans also organized the first strictly ethnic social club, the Aurora Turnverein, in 1861.[22]

The growth rate for Aurora was quite phenomenal, as Table 1 demonstrates. In spite of rapid change, the city managed to maintain a degree of order and control that was important in shaping and directing this growth. Thus, while many of the problems of ethnic, racial and class strife that troubled cities across the nation could be found in Aurora, the quality of life was high compared with many of her urban neighbors. For example, the C. B. & Q. was of supreme importance to the success and vitality of the city's economy. Yet entrepreneurs and capitalists used the railroad to create diversity in local manufacturing and business, so the railroad did not turn Aurora into a company town the way U. S. Steel did in Gary, Indiana. Similarly, Aurora never developed a single industrial district. Foundries, utilities, all types of businesses were dispersed throughout the city. Because the workers were not all crowded together in one section, Aurora did not take on the urban landscape of tenements and slum housing that became synonymous with rapid urban growth in cities like Chicago.[23]

This, then, is the setting of our "composite biography." African Americans began arriving into this environment of "public opinions, social notions, business methods, forms of government [and] standards of morality" while others of their race were enslaved in cities and on plantations in the South. How they were received in Aurora and how they responded to this environment has become, in turn, part of the cultural background to our lives today.

Total Population of Aurora[24]

Year	Population
1834	14
1850	1895 †
1860	6011 †
1870	11,192
1880	11,873
1890	19,688
1900	24,147
1910	29,807
1920	36,397

Table 1

† Census figures for 1850 and 1860 included all of Aurora Township, not the city alone.

-Chapter Two-
Strangers Among Strangers

Joseph Bora, a 53-year-old White male whose occupation is listed simply as "laborer," is an ordinary enough entry in the 1850 Federal Census of the population of Kane County, Illinois. Where in Aurora Township he and his wife Julia lived is not recorded, but the house was a full one, with eight daughters and one son. The family had moved from South Carolina to Illinois some few years earlier.[25] Generally speaking, a laborer moving to a prosperous and quickly expanding town of mills and railroads would be an unexceptional entry in the census. What sets this family apart is that also living in the house are Phoebe and Gill, the first two African Americans officially recorded as residents of Aurora.

There is at least one other candidate for this historical "first." In 1853, the Aurora Guardian ran the following article:

> *No little excitement was caused during the last week by the rumor that a colored man named Jerry, for many years a resident of this town, was missing, and fears were even entertained that he had been kidnapped. They are, however, groundless, as Jerry took a different route; probably having a suspicion that "the hounds were on his track," he took his departure for a free country, in the direction of the Northern Star, via the Underground Rail Road, which is in good running order.*[26]

Unfortunately, "many years" does not clearly indicate when he arrived. It only adds evidence that African Americans were beginning to arrive and stay in Aurora around 1850. What is clear from this report, however, is that African Americans were not entirely safe in Aurora.

Those who did not have protection from "the hounds" had to eventually move north to Canada.

So how did Phoebe and Gill come to live in Aurora? Details that can be confirmed are scarce (see Appendix). No occupation was listed for Phoebe. No last name was provided for either entry. Her birthplace was recorded as "unknown," and no age was given. The enumerator did record that Gill was born in Illinois and that he was, at the time, one year old. Both are listed as "free black." Apart from their names and status in the slavery system, the only information given was that Phoebe was a pauper.[27] One source defined paupers as those "over and under the self-supporting age, the crippled and sick in hospitals."[28] It is plausible that Phoebe was working in the Bora home as a servant. She may even have been legally bound to the Boras as an indentured servant due to her status as an indigent.

With no solid information available for Phoebe and Gill, it would be presumptuous to try to construct an explanation of how they arrived so far North, though the temptation is strong. Perhaps it would be useful instead to examine briefly the history of African Americans in Illinois. At least in this way, we may place these two pioneers in an historical context.

The story of African Americans in Illinois is varied and complex, dating back to well before statehood. Europeans, particularly the French, explored the Illinois Territory in order to expand the fur trade. The traders learned quickly from the native inhabitants the networks of lakes, rivers and streams that lead almost directly from the Gulf of Saint Lawrence to the Gulf of Mexico. Small trading posts sprang up at key locations along this natural highway system. Jean

Baptiste Pointe DuSable, a free Black man, began one such settlement on the southern end of Lake Michigan around 1790, which eventually grew into the City of Chicago.

The French introduced slavery to this region during these earliest days of settlement. Though Great Britain wrested control of North America from the French in 1763, a British concession in the treaty that closed the French and Indian or Seven Years War allowed the French inhabitants of Vincennes and Kaskaskia to keep their slaves. In 1779, during the American Revolution, the expeditionary force of George Rogers Clark captured the territory and claimed it for Virginia. The government of Virginia naturally agreed to protect the "rights and liberties" of the French slaveholders.[29]

In 1781, the newly formed United States began debating the legal status of the enormous area between the Mississippi and Ohio Rivers and the Great Lakes known simply as the Northwest Territory. Slavery was a pre-existing reality, at least in areas where the French had settled. Thus, when the issue of prohibiting slavery from the Territory arose, slaveholders in the region and across the South objected vehemently. In 1784, a committee led by Thomas Jefferson put forth a compromise that allowed slavery in the Territory until 1800, then phased it out. Much to Jefferson's surprise, his solution was roundly criticized and defeated. When the issue arose again in 1787 with a proposal to divide the Territory into as many as five new states, it seemed unlikely that the result would be different. However, Nathan Dane managed to attach Article 6, prohibiting slavery in the Northwest Territory, to the proposed Ordinance just prior to the vote. Congress was hurrying to adjourn and return home, and the Northwest Ordinance of 1787 was passed without debate, clearing the way for the admission of Ohio, Indiana, Illinois, Michigan and Wisconsin into the Union as free states.[30]

Slaveholders living in the region were outraged, and many began working to get Article 6 rescinded, or at least modified. Upon failing this, slaveholders in Indiana and Illinois set up systems of servitude that skirted the legal prohibition by tampering with the definition of slavery. Local laws permitted emigrating slave owners to bring their slaves to Illinois as indentured servants. All that was needed was the formality of a labor contract that outlined what was required of both parties. The master was to provide the basics of food, clothing and shelter. In return, male servants were bound to work until age thirty-five, and females until age twenty-eight. The law also gave masters nearly total control over their servants' disposition. It was no difficulty to coerce men and women who had been raised in bondage to White men, and who had no recognized legal rights, into signing such documents.[31]

Illinois was settled from south to north. During the last part of the eighteenth century and the beginning of the nineteenth century, the biggest settlements were in the area between the Ohio and Mississippi Rivers. The majority of newcomers to arrive and settle the Territory during this time were from southern Indiana, the Carolinas, Kentucky, Tennessee and Virginia.[32] Many of these settlers brought their slaves as servants, or to labor on their new farms. Even those who did not have slaves themselves were deeply inculcated in the system of slavery and accepted it.

When Illinois applied for statehood, there was little debate about what legal and political status African Americans would hold. Article 6 of the Northwest Ordinance was probably the only factor that prevented the Illinois Constitutional Convention from granting slavery legal standing. Because of that block, the delegates still had to cloak slavery within a system of indentured servitude.

> *Neither Slavery nor involuntary servitude shall hereafter be introduced into this state, otherwise than for the punishment of crimes, whereof the party shall have been duly convicted; nor shall any male person, arrived at the age of twenty-one years, nor female person, arrived at the age of eighteen years, be held to serve any person as a servant, under any indenture hereafter made, unless such person shall enter into such indenture while in a state of perfect freedom, and on condition of a bona fide consideration received or to be received for their service. Nor shall any indenture of any negro or mulatto hereafter made and executed out of this state, or if made in this state, where the term of service exceeds one year, be of the least validity, except those given in cases of apprenticeship.*[33]

The subtle key to the masquerade, according to Stephen Middleton, is the word "hereafter," which "indicates that convention delegates opposed only the introduction of slaves after 1818."[34] The important question skirted in the State Constitution is whether any Black man, woman or child living in Illinois in 1818 could enter into a contract "in a state of perfect freedom." The combination of an existing slave culture that demanded obedience from African Americans, a constitutionally protected system of long term servitude through indenture, and the denial of civil rights to anyone of color practically ensured that something very like slavery would flourish, in spite of the legal restrictions. In fact, many people registered slaves in open defiance of the Northwest Ordinance and the State Constitution, particularly in the southern end of the state. The Federal Census of 1810 registered 168 slaves in the Territory. In 1820, census takers recorded 917 slaves in Illinios, an increase of roughly 546 percent.[35]

Just one year after Illinois was accepted into the Union, the State Legislature passed its first set of "Black Laws." Slaves were required to carry a pass when travelling in the state. Free Blacks were required to show documents proving their claims and to register with the county clerk. To prevent southern slave owners from freeing their slaves in Illinois, a $1,000 bond was required for each individual released.[36] These and other restrictive ordinances were intended to control all African Americans living in the state and, more importantly, to make Illinois as unattractive as possible to free Blacks migrating from the South.

Settlement of the northern portion of Illinois began in earnest around 1830. Most of the people flooding into the region were from the northeastern United States. They brought with them their religion, their politics, and the abolitionism that grew from the merger of those forces. Many of these people were willing to risk their lives and property in breaking laws that they deemed abhorrent and sinful. While social unrest and political sniping pushed the country toward war, the renowned Underground Railroad network was expanding its operations in the sparsely populated areas of northern and central Illinois. Even after the Federal Fugitive Slave Law was passed, which imposed heavy penalties for assisting runaway slaves, people in northern Illinois, in cities like Aurora, winked at the law and fairly openly assisted slaves on the road to Canada and freedom. They also began political maneuverings, with an eye toward social reform and the eventual destruction of the slave culture.

The Federal Census of 1860 was taken in this tumultuous setting, with the smoldering hostility over issues surrounding slavery about to break into open warfare. While the information taken for this census was certainly more complete than in the 1850 Census, some valuable data were not included, including the informants' addresses. Furthermore, Census takers found only two African American households in Aurora in 1860, which does not provide a very good statistical base for this study. Even so, there are important facts to be gleaned and interesting historical issues raised even by this small sample.

One such issue is whether to interpret adulthood as a chronological age or as a cultural category based on independence, abilities and responsibilities? The censuses reveal numerous examples of African American children as young as thirteen employed full-time and part-time, and living independently as boarders or in the homes of their employers. Post-slavery African American culture may have considered teenagers adults, or poverty may have pushed children to take on extra obligations. For purposes of clarity and simplicity, this study marks adulthood chronologically, with twenty-one the age of majority.

The 1860 Census records twelve African American individuals living and working in Aurora. George Gillman, who was listed as a White man, and his wife Mary, who was listed as "mulatto," headed one family. Their four sons ranged between fourteen and three years of age. A forty-eight year old Black man named William Parker also lived in the house, perhaps as a boarder, though no relationship was given. The second household consisted of David Demery, his wife Julia, and four children between the ages of sixteen and two.

While the census did not include addresses, the Kane County Directory of 1858 listed David and Julia "Dimery" at LaSalle Street, between Main and New York.[37] This was not a terribly desirable

View looking west and south across Stolp Island. A note on the back of this photo indicates that Matilda Twiggs (spelled Triggs in some sources) lived in the house with the fenced garden on the far right. The location was not ideal; during floods the island was generally inundated with water. "Aunty" Twiggs, as she was often called, accepted a degree of risk in exchange for a house with land for her garden. It may have been close to her work, also. In 1868, she was working in the Evans Brothers Ice Cream Saloon, on nearby Fox Street.

From the collections of the Aurora Historical Society

location. The main line of the C. B. & Q. ran directly along that part of LaSalle, making this a dirty, noisy and somewhat dangerous area to raise a family. George Gillman's name does not appear in any Directories, so we have no basis to make any inferences about the neighborhood in which he and his family lived.

Of the five adults recorded in these two domestic arrangements, four were designated as employed in some form. Both of the men who headed their respective households were employed in unskilled positions. Gillman was recorded simply as a laborer, Demery as a whitewasher. Both of their wives worked as washerwomen, as did the Demerys' eldest daughter, Sarah, who was sixteen.[38]

One might expect that these families had moved to this industrial northern city from southern states. After all, at this time around ninety percent of African Americans lived in the South. However, the census data suggests that both families had lived in Illinois for some time. The 1860 Census records each of the Gillman children as having been born in Illinois. The oldest child was fourteen, which places the family in Illinois as early as 1846. Unfortunately, the information on the Demery children was incomplete in 1860. The 1870 Census confirms that the family had lived in Illinois since at least 1852. Sarah, who was twenty-six, was not recorded with the family in 1870, but all of the children still living at home were born in Illinois and the oldest was eighteen. Julia Demery was born in Illinois in 1820, and may have met David as he moved north from his home state of Tennessee.

For the millions of people held in slavery in the United States the Civil War brought about their release, but it also brought great disruption

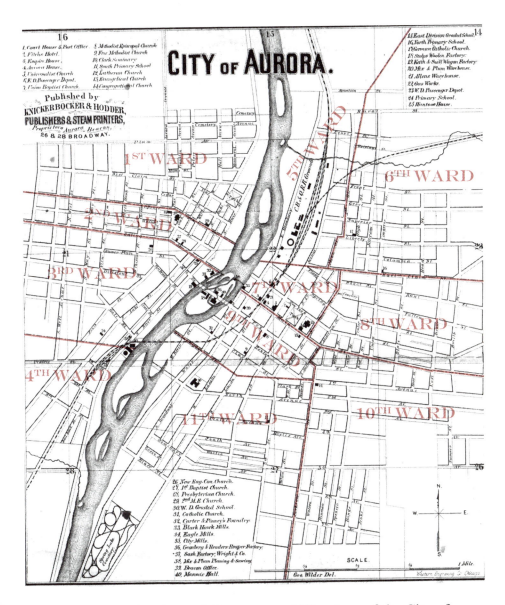

Aurora As It Is: First Annual Gazetteer and Directory of the City of Aurora. Aurora, IL: Knickerbocker & Hodder, 1868.

From the collections of the Aurora Historical Society

and questions of precisely what "freedom" meant to Black Americans. Readers of the <u>Aurora Beacon</u> were made aware of this uncertainty by a series of four articles that were submitted under the name of Andy Lee. The first, headed "Privileges and Views of Andy Lee A. C. of A. D.," appeared on 3 January 1867.

> *I have recently discovered that I am a part of the human race—that I have privileges. The Emancipation Proclamation and the late elections have sealed them to such as me. It is now my imperative duty to enter upon the enjoyment of the favors bestowed.*
>
> *I have long been conscious of slumbering powers. I am a blood name-sake of the two leading Confederate Generals, Andy Johnson and Robert Lee. I am an American citizen of African descent.*
>
> *Where shall my powers find play and display if not in the arena of politics? It is in politics that the human race has made the best time. I have not been idle. On my way up from slavery to glory I have seen that in politics men have done most, and women and American citizens of African descent, least. These things are now changed. From being the sill of society, (which was slavery), I have passed on to become a prominent plank in the platform of a party, (which was nigger)—on, to become the figure head of a gigantic rebellion, (which was contraband)—on, on to become a Member of the Legislature, (which is glory).*[39]

An extensive search through local, regional, state and national resources failed to locate an African American named Andy Lee writing or lecturing on African American civil rights or women's suffrage, both of which the articles extol. It is very likely that "Andy Lee" is a pseudonym. He may have been writing as a sort of Everyman. It is even possible that the author was a White man writing in the persona of a Black man to make a political point. In the end it does not matter much, because the author's insights remain valid. After generations of having their humanity denied on every level, African Americans were suddenly allotted a space in American life. How much room they would be given to allow their powers to "find play and display" was still an open question.

In spite of the pressure applied by Black and White abolitionists, Illinois did not rescind its Black Laws until the war was concluded in 1865, and even then much of Illinois remained harshly segregated. Nevertheless, when the most oppressive legal barriers finally came down, Illinois became a more attractive option for free Blacks trying to rebuild their lives. The Ninth Decennial Census reveals the first significant expansion in the African American population in Aurora. One hundred sixty-nine African Americans were living in Aurora in 1870. Table 2 shows that, as a percentage of the total, the overall impact of the jump in the Black population was negligible. The city, after all, had almost doubled in size (see Table 1, p. 29). Still, the town was certainly small enough for citizens to recognize the change, as Black faces became more common.

Aurora's African American Population, By Decade

Year	Individuals in Census	% of City Population
1850	2	.001
1860	12	.002
1870	169	.015
1880	231	.019
1900	280	.012
1910	299	.010
1920	638	.018

Table 2

With the growth in population, it becomes more reasonable to begin creating some statistical benchmarks, and comparing the data from decade to decade. In particular, the Federal Census is useful for tracking migration and settlement patterns; trends in employment and job opportunities; and changes in the basic level of education of the respondents. From these basic categories, we can make some inferences about the changing economic condition of Black migrants to Aurora, and witness the growth and progression of the African American community on its path toward glory.

By and large, the 1870 Census indicates that African Americans migrating into Aurora arrived as families. Only four of the forty-one households were adults living alone. In addition, four minors working as servants were listed independently, possibly because they were living in the homes of their employers. Most of the rest are clearly family units. Twelve heads of households were listed as boarders, renting a room or rooms in someone else's home, but the boarders included some families with children. There were also several entries showing multiple last names in a single dwelling, with no relationship given in explanation. These latter could be extended family groups.

It is important to know that the majority of these newcomers were families. It suggests permanence, an intention to settle and stay. Many of the former slaves who filtered north into Illinois during the Civil War and the years immediately following were the destitute elders, women and children who found themselves without support after emancipation. An announcement from the local auxiliary of the Freedmen's Aid Commission reported that some 3,000 African Americans were seeking aid in Quincy, Illinois, and that the majority were women and children.⁴⁰   Such large numbers in that insecure situation practically ensured that many of those people would be on the move again shortly. In contrast, Aurora's burgeoning Black population was building a safe and stable environment where they could raise their families.

Though the census does not allow us to directly trace where individuals or families lived prior to 1870, many in this post-war wave of migration appear to be recent arrivals. As Table 3 shows, the adults were born in nearly every state in the South, with Alabama, Kentucky, Virginia and Tennessee the most common. But sixty-seven entries, just less than forty percent of the total Black population of Aurora, were born in Illinois. Most of them were children born after Abraham Lincoln issued the Emancipation Proclamation on 1 January 1863. If we assume that the adults were mostly former slaves who never left the state where they were born until after emancipation, the natural conclusion is that the families had moved to Illinois some time recently—before the birth of these children.

These newcomers settled mainly into two wards: the Ninth along the Fox River in the southeast, and the Third along the River in the southwest. These two wards account for sixty percent of the African American population. If one includes the next two wards to the south of those, the Fourth and Eleventh, the figure rises to eighty-one percent of the total population of Blacks in Aurora, or one hundred thirty-six individuals. Of the remainder, seven percent lived in the First Ward, four percent in the Seventh Ward, and two percent in the Eighth. For the remaining six percent, the census was unclear as to their location.

Table 3

Place of Birth of African-American Inhabitants of Aurora, According to Federal Census Records

Place of Birth	1860	1870	1880	1900	1910	1920
Alabama		22	14	16	11	17
Arkansas			1		1	3
Canada		2		1		1
Florida						4
Georgia		2	2	2	2	11
Haiti		1				
Illinois	5	67	122	141	146	248
Indiana		2	4	4	8	24
Iowa			1	6	8	23
Kansas		4		2	1	11
Kentucky		14	16	17	36	106
Louisiana					2	9
Maine				1		1
Maryland		1	3	2	3	4
Massachusetts		2		1	1	
Mexico				1		
Michigan			2	4	2	6
Mississippi		5	1	3	6	18
Missouri		4	5	16	10	49
Nebraska						2
New York						2
North Carolina		2	4	2		4
North Dakota						1
Ohio		5	2	2	5	4
Oklahoma						4
Pennsylvania		1		2	1	1
South Carolina		2		2	1	1
Tennessee	2	12	28	32	20	47
Texas		2		1		7
Virginia	1	13	12	21	10	20
Washington, D.C.		4	2		1	
West Indies				1		
West Virginia		1		3		3
Wisconsin		1	2		1	3
Unknown	4		10	2	18	4
TOTAL	12	169	231	280	299	638

How should we interpret the obvious clustering of African Americans into these four wards? One possibility is that these neighborhoods grew from the desire of the Black migrants to "stick together." In Aurora, German, Luxembourg and French Canadian immigrants settled into distinct neighborhoods at first. Milton Gordon, in his study of immigration, concluded that most groups of immigrants initially "flocked together in 'colonies,' urban or rural," in an effort to reduce the sting of being strangers and to provide mutual aid.[41] Then again, it could be that racial bias on the part of the existing White population shunted incoming Black settlers into these neighborhoods and away from their own.

Evaluating the evidence is somewhat difficult due to the lack of specific information on employment. People generally tried to live near their work place, especially before the advent of streetcars and other mass transit options. Because of the one-dimensional nature of the employment opportunities that seem to have been available to Black men, one could argue that the local bias against giving African Americans jobs in the skilled trades and professions was a tool used with the intention of segregating them. Going by the entries in the census, it would appear that most of the Black men in Aurora were employed as laborers. Sadly, the locations of their employment are not available for comparison, which might indicate more reliably if discriminatory practices were used to keep African Americans ghettoized. The fact remains that the only skilled and semi-skilled positions listed for African Americans in this census are seven barbers, three of whom owned and operated their own shops. The 1870 Directory also listed a man named Edmund Coleman whose occupation was "stone cutter."[42] Only three women are listed as having any paid employment. All three were domestic servants.

It would be useful to compare previous employment and experience with the jobs that these men and women were doing, but such records simply do not exist. Generally speaking, many African Americans were coming from southern plantations, where they had labored in the production of cotton, tobacco, rice and sugar cane, and in the lumber and turpentine industries.[43]   None of these jobs were good preparation for work in factories or foundries. On the other hand, many plantations were nearly self-sufficient, which required some of the slaves to be trained artisans and mechanics. Another segment of the slave population provided personal services in the master's house, cooking and cleaning for the family, and waiting on them. It seems unlikely that none of these men and women had mechanical or other skills.

Black leaders and White philanthropists quickly identified the general lack of education among the African American population as an obstruction to the promise of freedom. Formal education, particularly the ability to read and write, was an important privilege that southern masters persistently denied to most slaves. It is not surprising, then, to find that thirty-two of the 169 African Americans counted in the 1870 Census for Aurora were listed as either unable to read, unable to write, or both. As one might expect, virtually all of the illiterate were adults who had likely been denied access to any formal education process as slaves; all but two were originally from southern states, and one of the two exceptions was from Washington, D.C. Only three entries listed as illiterate were under sixteen. The census also recorded that,

Broadway, looking north from the intersection at Fox (now Downer), c. 1870. Milton DeCoursey and Barton Manuel operated a barber shop in the Hill Building, shown in the foreground on the right side of the street.

From the collections of the Aurora Historical Society

of the twenty-nine children who were between the ages of six and sixteen, only ten had regularly attended school the previous year.

The population continued to expand at a fairly rapid rate and by 1880, 231 African Americans made their home in Aurora. As before, a sizable majority of the Black population were families. Only twenty-six entries in this census were for individuals: nine were boarding with other black families, eight were servants recorded in their employer's home, while nine were single heads of household. In addition, the African American population was young. Over half of the entries for this census were born in Illinois (See Table 3) and, true to the pattern set in 1870, seventy-eight percent of those listed as having been born in Illinois were under sixteen.

As the population expanded during the 1870s, African Americans continued to live primarily in the southern wards, with an increased concentration of settlement on the East Side. By the Census of 1880, only about twenty-two percent of African Americans for whom the address is known lived on the West Side. Most of that number still lived in the Third Ward. Over forty percent of the entire Black population lived in the Ninth, Tenth and Eleventh Wards, the southern third of the East Side. In a tantalizing contrast, the Seventh and Eighth Wards in the middle of the East Side also experienced growth (See map on page 54). The evidence is still pretty thin for speculation as to what was driving the choices, but it appears that African Americans were settling into distinct neighborhoods.

Employment and economic concerns remain likely factors in determining shifting settlement patterns. The Black population expanded on the East Side for the same reason German and Irish immigrants settled on the East Side; to be near the jobs. The more interesting question may be whether social influences are at work as well. Was financial and social status shaping the development of new neighborhoods? Is there evidence to support the inference that growing financial strength for some in the African American community was driving some of the demographic changes? While unskilled labor and service positions were still the norm, this census shows a gradual change in the jobs held by African Americans in Aurora. Census records for 1880 include skilled and semi-skilled positions, such as roofer, cook, upholsterer, and stone mason, in addition to barber. More women entered the work force in this census, mainly as servants in hotels and in private homes or as washerwomen, though Eva DeCoursey, daughter of barber Milton DeCoursey, was listed as a dress maker.

    The population growth increased the pool of illiterate and semi-literate people. Following the established pattern, people born in the South were much more likely to be illiterate. Of the fifty-five individuals listed as unable to read and/or write, only five were born in the North. Conversely, forty-seven were from the South, two from the District of Columbia and one did not know his birthplace.

    Education seems to have become more of a priority in the Black community. According to the 1880 Census, fifty-eight children between the ages of five and nineteen were attending school. Twenty-three were not. Annie Artis, a young woman who was still in school at the age of nineteen, is intriguing. The next oldest Black students recorded were fifteen. The data indicates that the norm in the African American community was to begin work around age sixteen. Either Annie was so

This photograph was entered in a contest under the title *"Aunty" Jackson's Reverie* in 1913. The camera captured the strength, the pain and the dignity of a woman familiar with labor. Women without experience or the opportunity to learn new skills worked primarily as servants. Carrie Jackson was a domestic in Caroline Potter's boarding house.

From the collections of the Aurora Historical Society

eager to learn that she was willing to sit in class with much younger children, or she was the first Black student to attend East Aurora High School. There are no attendance records to confirm this. Her name does not appear on the rolls of East High graduates.

The loss of the 1890 Census manuscript creates a large gap in the historical record. Between 1880 and 1900, the number of African Americans in Aurora increased by only twenty-one percent, a significant slowing of the pace compared with the previous two decades. This can be explained in large part by the phenomenal increase of European immigration during the same period. Aurora's population was booming, as Table 1 indicates (page 28). Thousands of immigrants from Germany, Eastern Europe and Scandinavia found their way to Aurora, flooding the labor market with skilled and unskilled hands. In 1900, African Americans throughout the North found themselves effectively locked out of the skilled trades, and even the service positions in hotels, restaurants and in private homes were being threatened.[44] With no economic incentive to draw them, migration from the South simply withered.

The Census of 1900 found 280 African Americans in Aurora. Migrants from Tennessee, Virginia and Missouri provided part of the increase, but as had been the case with the 1880 Census, the largest growth area was children born in Illinois.

The slowed growth in the African American population for the twenty years between censuses highlights the apparent progress in the acculturation process that was just beginning around 1880. One might have expected to find Aurora's African American residents still concentrated in the southern end of town. This was not the case. In fact, the Black population was pretty evenly spread through all of the wards.

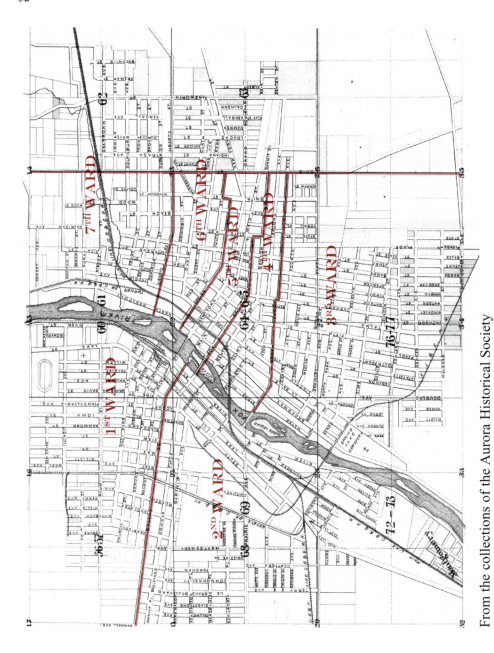

Atlas of Kane County, Illinois. Chicago: D. W. Ensign Co., 1892.

From the collections of the Aurora Historical Society

A change to the political map accounts for some of the even population distribution. In 1890, the City of Aurora reduced the number of wards from eleven to seven (See p. 52). Still, the redrawing of political boundaries is not the full explanation.

A significant number of African Americans lived on the edges of the city limits, outside of the ward boundaries, in 1900. The Directory of 1900-01, which indicated Black families and individuals by putting "(col)" after their names, recorded most of the households that the census listed as "Township" along the eastern edge of town, on Indiana Street around Pond, Claim and Kane. Given that finding, almost eighty percent of the African American population lived on the East Side, about the same as in 1880. But in 1900 most African Americans lived in the middle of the East Side, in the Fourth, Fifth and Sixth Wards. Even more importantly, the distribution of Black households was much more even than in 1880, with no ward holding more than sixteen percent. It would seem that the African American community was sorting itself out into economic classes, as was the rest of the city at this stage in its development. Black families were apparently exercising their ability to choose where they would live based on what they could afford.

The employment records support this hypothesis. More and more, African Americans broadened their horizons. Listed along with laborer, servant and porter in the occupations category are minister, plasterer, barber, shoe maker, brick maker, caterer, carpet weaver and mason. Alfred Lucas, listed as "patrol driver," was the first Black man to work for the city constabulary. Women continued to work mainly as servants and laundresses, but Emma Gigger's occupation was given as hairdresser.

At the start of the twentieth century, African Americans found themselves in competition for jobs with thousands of recent European immigrants. These two photos show one family at work around 1905. Identified as a caterer in the 1900 Census, Thomas Morton (front row, left side) is shown here in a group portrait of the Turkey Club. His daughter, Martha, is in the front row on another man's lap.

From the collections of the Aurora Historical Society

From the collections of the Aurora Historical Society

The 1905-06 City Directory identified Theodore Morton, son of Thomas Morton, as a porter in F. W. Woolson's Barber Shop at 69 South Broadway. The author has concluded that the man leaning in the doorway is Theodore. Woolson is likely the man seated in the center, and Gilbert Eberly is seated to his right.

Another interesting trend indicated in the 1900 Census is the reduction in illiteracy in the African American community. Though the population increased by twenty-one percent, the number of people registered as illiterate or semi-literate went down twenty-seven percent. Again, all but one of those listed as illiterate came from southern states. Furthermore, the youngest person in this category was thirty-four. Taken together, these numbers indicate that Black children were at least getting an education in the fundamentals.

The enumeration of 1910 uncovered a dramatic reduction in growth for the Black community. Combined with the slow pace of growth between the 1880 and 1900 Censuses, the 1910 Census seems to prove that, when making the decision to relocate, African Americans no longer felt that Aurora held the promise of economic benefit. News may have traveled south that European immigrants were monopolizing the job market. Or perhaps Chicago's much greater Black community, which grew from 30,000 to 44,000 between 1900 and 1910[45], acted as a magnet, attracting those that did venture into the area from the South. Whatever the cause, the population of African Americans in Aurora stayed almost level in the first decade of the twentieth century, officially rising by a mere nineteen individuals.

In spite of the sluggish pace of migration, the demographics continued to change, reinforcing the theory that at least some African Americans were gaining economic autonomy. A sizeable Black enclave developed in the First Ward. Just over thirty-percent of the Black population now lived on the West Side, though none lived in the fashionable, wealthy neighborhoods except for live-in servants. The Fourth and Fifth Wards remained important areas, as well. Black residents on the whole remained fairly evenly dispersed between the various wards.

As Aurora's economy expanded, Black men continued to make inroads in the employment opportunities available in the new businesses and industries. Samuel Bell was employed as an engineer for one of the local manufacturers. Rathbone and Sard Stove Works, the Wilcox Manufacturing Company, and the Chicago and Aurora Smelting and Refining Company all hired African Americans. African Americans were finding their way into the local stores and shops as well, primarily as teamsters and porters, but Charles Dyer was clerk in a dry goods store and Allen Lewis was a cabinet maker. A few women also made important breakthroughs. For example, Minnie Jackson was a teacher at an industrial school, Marie Muse taught in public school, and Frances Wallace opened her own dressmaker's shop.

African Americans, with much work, were beginning to gather some economic power. One sign of this growing financial strength was a notable increase in the number of homeowners. In 1900, the first time that the census recorded whether respondents owned or rented housing, only twenty-one African Americans owned their homes. Fifty were recorded as renters. In addition, at least ten were boarding with other families. In 1910, thirty-four were homeowners, and thirty-seven rented. The increase in home-ownership triggered a corresponding increase in boarders. The enumerators found thirty people boarding in other homes. Some families doubtless took advantage of their opportunities to defray the cost of home ownership. Moreover, boarding may have acted as a cultural and social safety net, deepening and strengthening ties within the African American community.

Photograph taken in an unknown Aurora saloon in 1905. The man behind the register wears a watch in the pocket of his waistcoat, a white shirt and a tie; the markers of middle class fashion.

From the collections of the Aurora Historical Society

The literacy rate also made a rapid improvement in this decade. By 1910 only ten individuals were recorded as illiterate. Those unable to read and write in the 1900 Census were generally between forty and eighty-five years old. Some of this population died in the following ten years; some moved away; some may have even learned to read and write. But while changing demographics may have contributed, the progress is a clear demonstration that access to public schools was creating a positive impact among African Americans in Aurora.

After practically leveling off around the turn of the century, Aurora's African American population ballooned to 638 individuals in 1920, more than double the figure from the 1910 Census. Migrants representing twenty-nine states from every point on the compass arrived in Aurora. This sudden growth spurt is part of the legacy of the "Great Migration," the designation given by historians to a massive shift of America's Black population that began after 1910. Vast numbers of African Americans moved from rural areas of the South, generally ending up in northern industrial centers like New York, Chicago, Detroit and Philadelphia. A variety of natural and artificial causes helped to create this momentous change.

It almost need not be mentioned that social conditions for African Americans in the South were atrocious, and worsening with time. The rising power of the Ku Klux Klan made lynching an almost daily occurrence, voting rights were nearly eliminated, and entrenched Jim Crow laws enforced segregation. However, these conditions had been prevailing for many years, and yet the majority of the Black population remained in the South. So what changed?

In 1912 and again in 1913, intense flooding in the South, particularly along the Mississippi River, destroyed crops and lowered land values. At the same time, a spreading infestation of the boll weevil was wreaking havoc on cotton growers, virtually wiping out entire harvests. While economic conditions worsened in the South, the more industrial North was experiencing a growing labor shortage. The threatening cloud of war in Europe had interrupted the tide of immigration from foreign ports. When the U.S. entered World War I in 1917, the increased need for production to supply the war effort and the introduction of the draft combined to strain the labor supply even further.[46]

As Robert Bruce Grant pointed out, however, such a mass movement cannot fairly be attributed to outside forces alone. Certainly African Americans had reasons to seek better opportunities. And just as certainly, all of the reasons cited above helped to build an atmosphere conducive to a mass migration. But in the end it remained for the people themselves to decide that it was in their best interests to give up the life they had known, and to cast their lot in the industrial North.

> *The tide of Negro migration, northward and cityward, is not to be fully explained as a blind flood started by the demands of war industry coupled with the shutting off of foreign migration, or by the pressure of poor crops coupled with increased social terrorism in certain sections of the South and Southwest. Neither labor demand, the boll weevil nor the Ku Klux Klan is a basic factor, however contributory any or all of them may have been. The wash and rush of this human tide on the beach line of the northern city centers is to be explained primarily in terms of a new vision of opportunity, of social and economic freedom, of a spirit to seize, even in the face of an extortionate and heavy tool [sic], a chance for the improvement of conditions.*[47]

Promoting this "new vision of opportunity" and encouraging African Americans to seize their new chance at economic freedom was the Chicago Defender, perhaps the most influential periodical published by and for African Americans in the early twentieth century. The Defender boldly reported the injustices and atrocities in the South, and actively encouraged migration north. Just as importantly, they helped establish the social framework that enabled people thinking about change to move toward that goal. The Defender published "help wanted" advertisements, and the office served as a liaison between companies and potential workers in the South. Such a great voice for change drawing people toward Chicago probably boosted Aurora's sudden growth as well.

Nationally, the shift in population centers was so sudden, so extensive, that the Bureau of the Census was not up to the challenge. The Census of 1920 is notorious for its undercount of African Americans. In Chicago, for example, the population exploded from 44,000 to 110,000.[48] In a smaller city like Aurora, where the change was far less dramatic, the enumerators' task was not as daunting. Presumably, the count is reasonably accurate.

Above and beyond the fact that Aurora's African American population more than doubled between 1910 and 1920, the pattern of settlement is once again of great interest. The population in the First Ward remained relatively steady, while the Second Ward just about doubled in size. The Third Ward also practically doubled in size. Meanwhile, the number of African Americans in the Fourth Ward dropped by half. The Fifth and Seventh Wards saw sizeable increases. But the real story was the Sixth Ward, which increased its Black population by a factor of ten, from twenty-six in 1910 to 268 in 1920. The Sixth Ward alone held forty-two percent of the total African American population (See map on page 51).

What caused this sudden influx into one area of the city, after several decades of fairly even distribution? That can be answered in one word: industry. As mentioned in the first chapter, while the West Side has always had some industry of its own, most of the large industrial and manufacturing businesses were located in the East. However, few Black workers had access to those industrial jobs. That is, until the draft began in 1917. For while Robert Bruce Grant was correct to observe that the great rush of African Americans toward the industrial north should be seen as thousands of individual acts of faith and defiance, the sudden availability of much higher wages from manufacturers was a vital contributory factor. Carter G. Woodson's observations on the situation across the North echo strongly the circumstances in Aurora.

> *Negro laborers, who once went from city to city, seeking such employment as trades unions left to them, can work even as skilled laborers throughout the North. Women of color formerly excluded from domestic service by foreign maids are now in demand. Many mills and factories which Negroes were prohibited from entering a few years ago are now bidding for their labor. Railroads cannot find help to keep their property in repair, contractors fall short of their plans for failure to hold mechanics drawn into the industrial boom and the United States Government has had to advertise for men to hasten to the preparation for war.*[49]

For the first time, a significant number of Black men were landing skilled positions in the railroad yards and shops, and with other industries in town, most of which were in the northeastern section in and around the Sixth Ward. Meanwhile, Black women, who had worked almost exclusively in service positions, found that the doors of the factories were even opened to them. Several women are listed as machine operators in garment factories. As their jobs improved, these men and women moved into better housing that was closer to their work.

Not surprisingly, in this boom town atmosphere, the number of renters and boarders, and the number of servants listed in the homes of their employers, is quite large. However, the number of home owners also grew at an impressive rate, rising from thirty-four to sixty-three. More significantly, migration of African Americans to Aurora remained family oriented. Nationally, single Black men were the most likely to move in search of a better life, tempted by scouts sent South by desperate employers to recruit any warm body. But if a better offer came along, these employees might bolt. Having found good work and a stable life, a man was far less likely to uproot an entire family to chase other employment offers. The data suggests that most of the African American community in Aurora was living in family units. For employers in Aurora, this meant an enviable stability in their work force.

-Chapter 3-
Liberal Ideals, Racial Biases

Aurora was a firmly established town by the time Phoebe and Gill, our two Black pioneers, arrived around 1850. It was an important and eventful time in national and local history. Sentiment was growing in the North to find some means of abolishing slavery. Slave states in the South fought at every available opportunity to maintain the system on which they had built their economies. The rising tide of emotion reached its crest in Aurora in 1854. Slavery was taking central place in the political debates and the Whigs and the Democrats, the two main parties at the time, were trying to stake out favorable positions.

Locally, Kane County, which had been solidly Democratic in the Presidential election of 1836, was switching allegiance to the Whig Party because of the perceived influence of slavery over the Democrats. However, neither party could find unity on the issue of slavery, and both resorted to legal compromises in the face of building pressure. In 1850, the political landscape was being shaped, literally, by a piece of legislation known as the Missouri Compromise. Forged in 1820, it created a fragile balance of power between the slave and free states by dividing the remaining land from the Louisiana Purchase. States created north of 36°30' North Latitude would be free; south of that line slavery would be legal. Another series of Congressional compromises culminated in the Fugitive Slave Law of 1851, a federal law that imposed heavy fines on those caught helping escaped slaves and extended slave-owners' powers to retrieve runaways even in northern states. Opposition to this law splintered nearly all party alliance in

Aurora. Passage of the Kansas-Nebraska Act three years later repealed the Missouri Compromise and opened the possibility for the expansion of slavery throughout the Western Territories. The destruction of the temporary balance that had been achieved through the Missouri Compromise sounded the death knell for the Whig Party in America.

In Kane County, Whigs disillusioned with their party's inability to stop the expansion of slavery much less eliminate the "peculiar institution" joined with "Free Soil" Democrats, who opposed slavery because it threatened the ability of individual farmers and laborers to compete in the market. In search of a new path, an authorized "People's" convention, held in the First Congregational Church of Aurora the evening of 20 September 1854, established a solidly anti-slavery political platform for a new party, which the delegates named "Republican."[50]

The choice of meeting places was certainly appropriate and meaningful. The building in which they met was the first church building erected in Aurora. It had been founded in 1841 as a Presbyterian Church. However, strong abolitionist feelings in the congregation, encouraged first by Reverend J. A. Hallock and then stoked into open passion by Reverend W. L. Parsons, created a rift with the national leadership. When the General Assembly of the Presbyterian Church failed to condemn slavery in 1848, the congregation withdrew themselves from the Presbytery and aligned themselves with the Congregationalists.[51]

During the next few years, Reverend Hallock and several members of the church actively promoted and assisted in the network of safe houses known as the Underground Railroad. In a history of the

From the collections of the Aurora Historical Society

Looking east on Main Street (now Galena), 1866. Three historic churches are visible. The one to the left, with its steeple barely above the trees, was First Congregational Church from 1841 to 1857. This was the site of the "People's" convention in 1854 that was the start of Republican politics in the area, and the venue for a debate that featured Frederick Douglass. In 1856, First Congregational built the stone building with the pointed steeple in the background. Both buildings were on the Underground Railroad. The building with the incomplete steeple was the Universalist Church. Rev. J.G. Bartholomew preached a fiery anti-slavery sermon from its pulpit. A copy of that sermon survives in the A.H.S. archive.

church, Charles Wheaton recorded that "about town, the church was known as the 'Union Depot.'"[52]

When President Fillmore signed the Fugitive Slave Bill into law in 1850, the people of the First Congregational Church "condemned and repudiated [the law's] principles." The assembly produced a set of resolutions openly stating their belief that "the law of benevolence, the law of God, and the principles of Christianity are the higher law which we are bound to obey in opposition to all human authority."[53] In short, the proclamation gave notice that they had no intention of obeying or enforcing this particular edict from Washington.

While the Congregationalists were among the few in Aurora to stand in open and militant defiance at this time, individuals throughout the town quietly undermined the Fugitive Slave Law in their own ways. Some continued to shelter refugees bound for freedom in Canada, using the Underground Railroad. The so-called "conductors" actively aiding and transporting fugitives on to the next safe house were small in number and secretive, to protect themselves and their "passengers" from slave hunters. However, the system also relied on assistance from sympathetic people, or at the very least tacit approval and non-interference by local officials and neighbors.

John J. Wagner and his wife, Laura, were key participants in the local network. Recalling the operation years later, the Wagner's children would say that fugitives generally arrived under cover of darkness. Maria, to her mother's left in the portrait on page 69, remembered getting up in the night to cook meals for those her family was taught to refer to as "gentlemen of color." The family fed and sheltered them in their house and barn through the following day. When the sun went down again, Mr. Wagner would transport them to the next station in his wagon.⁵⁴

Given the political temperament of the Whig Party in Kane County, it is not surprising to find that the editor of the local Whig newspaper, the <u>Beacon</u>, was an outspoken critic of slavery and a supporter of the abolitionist movement. More significant are articles found in the <u>Guardian</u>, the local organ of the Democrats. The <u>Guardian</u> occasionally broke from the party ranks to brazenly voice its support for the Underground Railroad and abolition. Two articles that appeared on the front page on Wednesday, 23 February 1853, demonstrate the <u>Guardian</u>'s editorial stance. The first, reprinted from the <u>New York Tribune</u>, discussed the subjects of emancipation and colonization. The item closed by saying:

> *We have no desire to provoke or revive a wrangle with any one, but, while we are in favor of the termination of all human slavery at the earliest possible day, and protest against making the removal of the blacks to Africa a condition of their liberation, we nevertheless believe the colonization cause a noble and hopeful one, and regard its progress with satisfaction. The timid conservative who cries "No abolition without colonization!" and the rabid abolitionist who retorts "No colonization til the blacks are all emancipated!" are in our eyes equally mulish and irrational. Let all be emancipated as fast as possible, whether colonized or not, and let all who will be colonized, though others should not be emancipated. In this perverse world, we must do whatever good we can, without waiting until we can do all we would.*⁵⁵

The second article reported the outcome of the Illinois Senate's vote on a bill "to prohibit the immigration of free negroes in the State." Referring to the Senators who voted in favor of the bill, the editor expressed pride and relief "that Kane County had no one named among

The John J. Wagner Family, portrait by Sheldon Peck, c. 1845. As a symbol of the family's anti-slavery beliefs Peck placed the Western Citizen, an abolitionist newspaper with a radical political agenda, in Mr. Wagner's hand.

From the collections of the Aurora Historical Society. Photo by Michael Tropea.

that infamous thirteen," and suggested that "the present Legislature . . . has retreated toward the dark ages in legislation for the colored man."[56]

Yet another item printed by the <u>Guardian</u> reported "that 17 passengers passed through this place on the 'U. G. R. R.' and we saw one, solitary and alone, making for the depot about car time; and one Tuesday, in open daylight. The Chicago paper announces their arrival in that city and says they were immediately forwarded to the land of the free."[57] The <u>Guardian</u> also got some of its reports directly through this clandestine network, according to the editor of the rival town press.

> *The Aurora Guardian occasionally has items of news which it purports to receive per* **Underground Railroad**. *It happens quite often that news received at Chicago by telegraph, and published in the papers of Friday, appears in the Guardian of Thursday date. Steamships and telegraphic communications traverse the earth's surface, while we presume the U.G.R.R. passes directly through the earth's center, and that the advantages possessed by our contemporary are attributable to a connection in some way with this new* **cut-off**.[58] *[Emphasis his]*

In addition to private attempts to undermine the law and the open approval of these efforts by the principal newspapers, local political forces were in motion that would quickly bring sweeping change to the entire country. An article in the <u>Aurora Beacon</u> announced the results of a meeting of the Whigs of Kane County, held on 10 August 1850. After the assembly had nominated delegates to attend the upcoming Whig Congressional Convention in Joliet, the following resolutions were passed:

> *Resolved, That we are entirely and uncompromisingly opposed to the extension of slavery in any manner, whether by the annexation to slave holding Texas, of territory now free, or by admission to the Union of Territory already acquired, without an express prohibition of Slavery, either in*

> *the Constitution of each new State, asking admission, or in the Act of Congress providing for such admission.*
>
> *Resolved, That in the strong and explicit language of Daniel Webster, "our opposition to the increase of Slavery in this country, or increase of Slave representation in Congress, is general and universal. It has no reference to the lines of latitude or points of the compass. . . . We shall oppose all such extension and all such increase, in all places, at all times, under all circumstances, even against all inducements, against all combinations, against all compromise."*[59]

By 1854, the local papers felt free to declare that "the 'fugitive slave law' is in full force in Illinois—we don't mean the one passed at Washington but the other, passed by the people, that if the slave owners want their runaway darkies catched, they can do it themselves . . . . We venture to say that since the passage of the Fugitive Slave Act, more slaves get to Canada by half than before."

When the Kansas-Nebraska bill was passed that same year, a new firestorm of protest swept through Kane County that defied political bounds. Furious Whigs and "Free Soil" Democrats deplored the action. In Aurora, a special debate was scheduled pitting Senator Stephen Douglas, who crafted the final compromise, against Frederick Douglass, the brilliant author, orator and abolitionist. However, when the two men arrived, both were so ill that they were taken immediately from the train station to their quarters, and the event was cancelled. The crowd that had gathered was not to be denied. They called Frederick Douglass out, and convinced him to speak. A man from the Senator's camp endeavored to open the debate with a defense of Stephen Douglas. The staunchly abolitionist crowd, however, was unwilling to listen for long. A fight broke out that, according to one account, ended with Benjamin Franklin Parks, a local man known for his Democratic sympathies, being physically ejected from the hall through a window. Parks later denied that version of events. Some time after this melee, Senator Douglas was moved to comment from the relative safety of Springfield that "Kane County is the asylum of all the abolitionists."[61]

The Democratic Party in Kane County was hopelessly split over the issue of slavery, and two separate congressional conventions were held, with each nominating its own candidates. Kane County's Whigs, meanwhile, decided to hold their congressional convention in Aurora on 20 September 1854. Before that date, however, a mass meeting of all those "opposed to the aggression of the slave power," regardless of party affiliation, was called for in a petition signed by three hundred people.[62] The rules of American politics were about to change.

The mass meeting, held in the court house of neighboring Geneva, Illinois, produced a set of resolutions among which was the following:

> *Resolved: That the black laws of the state are unconstitutional, inhuman and barbarous; and it shall be [the] principal object of this organization to secure their repeal.*

This meeting was followed with a county convention, at which the delegates, an even mixture of Whigs and Democrats, crafted a platform and selected delegates to send to a "People's" Congressional Convention that was scheduled to open in Aurora on the same day as the Whig Convention. County conventions around northern Illinois adopted similar resolutions, and selected representatives to send to Aurora.[63]

On 20 September 1854, 207 delegates convened in the First Congregational Church. During the next few days, the People's Convention and the Whig Convention held several conferences, during which delegates from both sides debated the subject of fusion. However, no agreement could be reached, and the idea was voted down. Instead, the People's convention took the name Republican, and unanimously endorsed a "radical, concise and comprehensive platform," which "declared that the Republican party was pledged never to admit another slave state into the Union, and also that it was pledged to prohibit slavery in all the territories of the United States, not only all that we then had, but all that we should thereafter acquire, and to repeal, unconditionally, the fugitive slave law, abolish slavery in the District of Columbia, and prohibit the slave trade between the different states."[64]

Contrary to local lore, this convention was not the first to use the name "Republican." In February of 1854, even before the Kansas-Nebraska Bill had been signed into law, a mass meeting called in Ripon, Wisconsin suggested the name when the attendant Whigs and Democrats threatened to withdraw from their respective parties if the law went into effect. This event is generally accepted as the birth of the Republican Party. On 6 July 1854, a convention at Jackson, Michigan became the first organized meeting of the Republican Party.

Although Aurora is not granted the historical title "birthplace of the Republican Party," this convention was, without question, a momentous step in the party's development. The delegates passed a declarative set of resolutions stating a political agenda under the name Republican. The radical nature of the platform adopted in Aurora reflected the aggressively abolitionist sentiment of this city, and Kane County in general, prior to the Civil War. When war erupted, Illinois quickly rallied and sent some of the first troops to Washington, and by war's end, roughly one third of the adult male population of Aurora had fought in the Union army. But what inspired this strident effort?

Furthermore, how did these same people react once the abstract concept of runaways fleeing slave catchers became the reality of people who wanted to move in as neighbors?

Given the small number of African American residents in Aurora during the period covered by the 1850 and 1860 Censuses, there is a strong likelihood that the majority of residents in Aurora had little or no personal contact with the people whose liberty they were trying to achieve. And yet, there was such visceral emotion displayed over the issues surrounding slavery. What caused these people, so far removed from the realities of slavery, to feel such personal involvement?

To people in Aurora, as in other cities and towns across the North, slavery was a moral and religious issue with clear consequences for the country and themselves. The Reverend J. G. Bartholomew, pastor of the Universalist Church in Aurora, gave a sermon in 1859 in which he extolled the attempt by the late John Brown to start a slave insurrection, and challenged his listeners to see in Brown's controversial actions "the warning voices of the outraged law of right." Bartholomew insisted that the infamous political compromises to "slave power" had led only to betrayal and more compromises. Brown's raid on Harper's Ferry may have been "rash," but his motive was righteous. "We may call it what we will--madness, fanaticism, or treason--God is speaking in this event, and it becomes his servants to listen and obey."[66]

Throughout this treatise, Bartholomew attempted to get his White audience to feel common interest with the slaves. In that effort, he made the cause of freeing Black slaves in the South simply one aspect of the ultimate goal. The larger aim, barely submerged in the text, was to restore to the descendants of Puritanism the authority and power that he claimed the slave states had stolen by degrees. Abolishing slavery was a means to that end. Truly, the objective was to win freedom, but it was the freedom of Aurorans that received the most attention, at least in this sermon.

To Bartholomew, the "cause of freedom for the slave is one that appeals to every human soul. It is a cause you can carry home with you, and take to your closets."[67] The issue of slavery was a crusade that almost anyone could support on some level, even if it was only out of personal interest. He implored his listeners, "As you love your freedom, the dearest gift of God--as you love your children and your homes; as you love humanity, and regard their rights: as you love the Saviour, and the cause for which he died upon the cross--as you respect the Higher Law, and revere the sacred name of God, never compromise with that great wrong."[68]

The reason one should never compromise with slavery, Bartholomew revealed, was that "we are ourselves slaves." "Look at Slavery," he urged, "not in its effect upon the slave or the master—we know how it degrades them; how it curses the very soil where it exists—not upon them, but upon ourselves; for its dark shadow falls upon the light of Freedom in our northern homes." He continued:

> *See how it degrades our churches. It muzzles the mouths of our preachers, and binds our ecclesiastical cowards in shameful silence. Look at the American Tract Society. It dare not publish a tract against that 'sum of all villainies,' though taught by that Divine word which they pretend to preach, to 'remember those in bonds as bound with them,' that great council of religious teachers, professing to follow him who came to preach deliverance to the captive, to break every yoke, and let the oppressed go free, dare not utter one word in behalf of the poor slave.*

> *See, too, how it degrades our Politics. It would compel us to yield up our rights in the free territory, to the monopoly of 350,000 slave holders, and shut out our freemen by the iron door of slavery, from the most valuable lands in our country. It would bind us down by the 'Fugitive Slave Bill'. . . compel us to leave our employment, leave our quiet homes, and go out at the command of a slave driver, and chase a poor fugitive, fleeing to secure what God intended for every person, white or black--life and liberty."*[69]

John Brown was a hero, then, because it was "not merely the interest of the Black man that was involved in that struggle at Harper's Ferry. It was our own interests, and the interests of our wives and children."

"Family values" is not a new issue in the political history of the Republican Party. Harriet Beecher Stowe's <u>Uncle Tom's Cabin</u> resonated with the emotionally rich motif of family, showing the effects that slavery had on both Black and White families. Concepts of family, personal responsibility, and morality, together with sizable doses of religious zeal, appear in virtually every anti-slavery speech, sermon, pamphlet and newspaper article. These simple themes carried strong emotional impact, and the abolitionist movement skillfully employed them to their advantage at every opportunity.

Still, it was much easier to win the support of middle-class and working-class Whites by showing them the effect that slavery had on them—even to the virtual exclusion of slaves from the equation. The majority of Aurorans who heard this sermon, or who later purchased the published text, would have agreed that the enslavement of millions of men, women and children as labor for an elite group of planters was morally reprehensible. However, gaining sympathy for the slaves was only one step toward enlisting active support. The climax of this sermon, quoted above, are arguments against the Fugitive Slave Law and the Kansas-Nebraska Act based on the more moderate political views of the "Free Soil" Democrats. By illustrating effects that the slavery system was having on the country, including the economic impact on northern workers who could not compete with a system based on slave labor, Reverend Bartholomew was more likely to get his White, Protestant audience to recognize common interest with the slaves. This, in turn, motivated them to seek the destruction of the system of slavery by whatever means available.

It is important to note that Rev. Bartholomew barely spoke of slaves in this treatise against slavery. Few White people, North or South, considered African Americans their equals. Two racial theories dominated the social, religious and scientific thought of the late nineteenth and early twentieth century. On the one hand, African Americans were perceived as docile, stupid (or at least ignorant), contented with their lot but in need of "raising up." Conversely, the other view posited that they were animalistic, vicious and depraved. Proponents of this second theory worried that the end result of emancipation would be the subversion of the existing culture by the Black race. Implicit in both assessments was an innate inferiority. The fact that the two philosophies were fundamentally contradictory was simply ignored. By keeping the reality of the slaves themselves somewhat vague, Bartholomew averted controversy over what was to be done with the slaves after setting them free.

The total population of Aurora in 1860 was 6,011, with only twelve African Americans. Put another way, African Americans were in the minority by about 500 to one. And since all twelve known Black residents lived in two houses, it is unlikely that the daily lives of most Aurorans were impacted by this small enclave. For those in town who did not have contact with either the Demery or the Gillman family, or who did not participate with the Underground Railroad, what shaped their understanding of African Americans and African American culture? What were their preconceptions?

The press was the primary source of information that brought African Americans into the consciousness of Aurorans. Unfortunately, contemporary accounts in the <u>Beacon</u> are virtually silent on the subject of migration into Aurora by African Americans, even during periods of great growth. Broad political topics were treated in detail during the decade following the Civil War. Stories off the wire illustrating the continued violence against southern Blacks, editorials articulating the political rights of African Americans, and articles reporting the progress of adjustment from slavery to citizenship, all combined to feed the continued interest that Aurorans felt in these issues. Occasionally, as we shall see, articles about local events also found their way into the pages of the <u>Beacon</u>. But these stories gradually disappeared and were replaced by jokes and cartoons depicting stereotypical "southern negroes" of the Reconstruction.

Disarray and turmoil followed hard on the heels of the Emancipation Proclamation. For centuries, African Americans had been denied many of the most basic human rights. Therefore, when liberation finally came, the desire to experience freedom was strong. Many African Americans chose to express their freedom, and simultaneously test the limits of that freedom, by picking up and moving. However, only a statistically small number moved North at first. Many began searching for family members and loved ones from whom they had been separated. Others exchanged their rural roots for the urban centers of the South. The few that did leave the region tended to move west, across the Mississippi.[73]

Both the army and the Federal government were caught unprepared for the mass movements of freed slaves, and African Americans frequently discovered that the basic needs of life were unavailable. Benevolent societies attempted to fill the void. Very quickly, these groups realized that the controversial question of what was to become of the freedmen was going to be a central issue of their efforts.

In November of 1864, almost two years after President Lincoln announced the Emancipation Proclamation, an article appeared in the Beacon announcing a fund raising event for the North Western Freedmen's Aid Commission (NWFAC), which began:

> *By one of those revolutions, which in the providence of Him who ruleth in the kingdoms of men, have from time to time taken place among the nations of the earth, the existing prejudices of many generations have been swept away, and an oppressed, downtrodden, and despised race, have emerged from the bondage and darkness of slavery, into the glorious light of Freedom.*
>
> *During the progress of the present contest for civil liberty, a great advance has been made towards the redemption of the colored race, and their elevation in the scale of humanity. The minds of men have gradually been enlightened; and now the right of the negro to be free, is very generally acknowledged.*[74]

But what, the author asked, was to become of the slaves after freedom? "It remains with [the American people] to decide the question of whether the slaves shall be freed, only to increase the already overflowing tide of ignorance and degradation in our country, which has ever prevailed to a great extent among the foreign born immigrants to our shores, or whether they shall be educated, and become enlightened members of society, fitted to provide for themselves and attain to positions of respectability in community."[75] The NWFAC chose the latter as its mission.

The article continued by defending the work of the Commission, and explaining why it was the patriotic duty of all "lovers of freedom" to assist in the cause. The author's main argument was that the freedmen were lightening the burden of the war. "There are now in the field two hundred thousand colored troops, thereby exempting from draft an equal number of white citizens." Furthermore, he claimed, "these colored soldiers do the work that would fall upon their White comrades in arms; they fight beside them, they shed their blood and lay down their lives."[76]

In return for their loyalty and sacrifice, the NWFAC wished to "improve the circumstances thus brought about in God's providence." They provided shelter, food and clothing to the women, children and elderly left behind by those who enlisted, making it possible for them to serve (in place of White men, remember). The Commission also provided education and religious training to prepare the free Blacks for life after slavery, so that they would not become a burden on society.[77]

In March of 1865, the newly formed Freedmen's Aid Society (FAS) announced through the Beacon their intention to assist this work.

> *The object of this Society is to solicit contributions in money, clothing, bedding, cooking and housekeeping utensils, such as are laid aside by their owners, and whatever else may aid the thousands of Freedmen, who, in the providence of God, are cast in different places in the North, in a destitute condition.*[78]

The FAS was entirely involved in securing money and supplies for the parent organization, the Northwestern Freedmen's Aid Commission. For the women who headed this local chapter, mainly the wives of prominent men in city business and government, helping the "freedmen" was both patriotic and altruistic. Like Reverend Bartholomew before her, the author of this announcement used the potent messages of Protestantism to put moral force behind a social/political crusade. This time, Christian charity and the Golden Rule provided the motivation. Gathering clothes, money and supplies for the refugees from the South enabled contributors to the Freedmen's Aid Society to "show our love to Christ and to his cause, by 'feeding and clothing him in the person of his afflicted poor.'"[79]

In the course of pleading for understanding and assistance, however, the author reveals a subtle cross-current of racial bias in her own understanding of the Black men and women for whom the Freedmen's Aid Society is laboring. A patronizing sense of noblesse oblige permeates her worldview. The negro, she asserts, is in "a plastic state…when our Christianity and our civilization can do more to raise him up to the dignity of liberty and manhood than in any other, and in all future times. They are now as untaught children, and need a guardian's care and friendly assistance."[80] Modern ears process blanket references to "the negro" as childlike and allusions to a general lack of morals and civilization among African Americans differently than the original audience. Still, though the author's intent was by no means malicious, it is important to point out that such language offers a clue to the range of thought and preconceptions about African Americans current in Aurora as the Civil War neared its end.

In subsequent months, regular progress reports of both the Freedmen's Aid Society and its parent organization, the North Western Freedmen's Aid Commission, appeared in the local press, showing that the plight of African Americans in their "new and embarrassing condition" continued to concern people in Aurora.[81] These reports provide an interesting opportunity for comparison. The regional commission gave considerable credit to the Black men and women they were assisting for improving their own lives, stressing in its reports that the continued success and results were due in large part to the "great eagerness for useful knowledge shown by this people" and their "remarkable eagerness to follow any honorable occupation."[82] In contrast, the group from Aurora, whose experiences probably included little or no direct daily contact with African Americans, assigned the credit to the "Yankee 'school marm' with her spelling book," because "the neatness, the energy, the refinement, and the culture of this teacher, is placing before the freedmen—an imitative race—an example that will leave impressions deep and lasting."[83]

The fact that the women of the Freedman's Aid Society worked on behalf of African Americans, who were in truth a "despised race," must not be ignored. Their conscience called them to action and they responded with zeal in defense of the basic rights of African Americans. "There is a disposition to say of the 'nigger,' as they call him, 'Let him paddle his own canoe.' A party—and they are mere scoffers, too—now say to us: 'You told us if he (the nigger) were free, he would take care of himself; now let him do it.'"[84] In spite of the fact that the tone of this rhetorical argument makes the Society's cause sound like a burden, and seems to assume that African Americans cannot take care of themselves, the underlying assumption is profound. These women are proclaiming that the freedmen should not be cut loose to paddle alone, that they must be recognized and accepted as part of American society. Of course, there can be little doubt that "the nigger" would occupy the lowest rung on the social ladder.

The editorial policy of the <u>Beacon</u> was firmly on the side of equality, even to the extent of appearing naive in some cases. In 1865, the <u>Beacon</u> appealed for suffrage for African Americans. Granted, the writer was concerned mainly with the threat posed by the reintroduction of Southerners into the political system, and hoped that African Americans would continue to tip the balance of political power toward the Republican Party. As noted earlier, identification of mutual benefit was often the key to local support for the causes of African Americans. However, he also allowed that "the Negro" was loyal and deserving, and concluded, "It is an absolute necessity that the emancipated blacks be admitted to vote, if the solemn pledges made to them are to be sacredly fulfilled."[85]

Three years before the ratification of the Fifteenth Amendment to the Constitution of the United States, the editors of the <u>Beacon</u> were demanding that the Illinois legislature remove from the State Constitution the distinction of race as a qualification on voting. In this instance, enlightened Republican ideology was the motivation.

> *We are in favor of the American principle of **democracy** in its broadest and most literal sense. The doctrine of **the people** ruling should be narrowed by no class restrictions or odious distinctions. It should be applied and carried out in the fullness and broadness of its definition in the Declaration of Independence. 'All men are born free and equal'—and under a free government, formed and maintained by **the people**, 'all men' should be deemed to be 'equal' before the*

law, in their political as well as civil rights and privileges.[86] [Emphasis his]

Never was the editor as confident of final victory in the fight for equality as he was in announcing the ratification of the Fifteenth Amendment on 16 February, 1870. "The end has come," he announced. "The long struggle over the negro question is over." With historical hindsight in our favor, it is clear that this pronouncement was premature. But he believed that bringing African Americans (men only, of course) fully into the political system eliminated the need for special protective legislation. The Amendment would ensure fairness and access to the democratic process, and the process would ensure an equal protection through the law. There would be no more debate on the rights of Blacks versus Whites; only on the rights of Americans.[87]

In addition to suffrage, the Beacon championed the cause of education among the Black population, as the following article about a city almost 200 miles away illustrates:

It is sad indeed, to see that the bigoted hatred of race which so long cursed our land, is not yet eradicated by the stern events of the last decade. The enfranchisement of the colored man has made a great mass of ignorant men voters, and participants in the government of our nation. They feel their own defects, and with as few average instances as there would be among almost any other race, are striving to elevate themselves, so that they may intelligently, honestly and honorably, discharge the duties devolved upon them. While thus striving to help themselves, it would seem the part of common sense, and humanity, as well of self interest, for the white man to aid them in every possible way. No man can safely elevate himself by keeping another beneath him; neither will he the sooner reach any desirable good by casting impediments in the way of his equal, far less his inferior. Still, we almost every day hear of foolish attempts to hinder the education of the negro. But a few days since a young colored lady, of large mental capacity, and excellent *scholarship, was admitted to the Quincy High School, when 37 white girls left school, and only returned when the colored girl was **expelled**. [Rebels] can sit in the United States Senate, but no one of colored skin can attend the Quincy High School. And but last week, the physicians and surgeons came to Washington in great force, and for days fought over some local quarrels among the doctors of the District of Columbia, turning upon the point whether or not some well educated, skillful and successful colored physicians and colored surgeons should be recognized, all terminating in a temporary victory for the bigots. The negroes know and appreciate all this, and they are wiser than their opponents in a determination to continue in the efforts for education, with certainty of success.*[88] *[Emphasis his]*

Aurora's school system was undeniably progressive. In 1851, when the rest of Illinois and much of the nation still based education on a family's ability to pay, Aurora introduced a system of free schools. In policy and in practice, any child in the district could attend school. The best evidence that exists to verify that Aurorans practiced what the Beacon preached in terms of educational opportunities can be found in the census returns that we examined in chapter two. Naturally, we cannot take for granted that the students were treated equally in the school system. Still, there is certainly evidence that African American children in Aurora were seizing the opportunities presented to them to educate themselves, which was an opportunity few of their elders had been given.

Perhaps what best describes the prevalent attitude of Aurorans concerning African Americans during this early period, when Black families and individuals were just beginning to arrive as fellow citizens, is paternalism. It would be terribly unfair to gloss over the concern that many in the White community obviously felt. The local abolitionists

New York Street School, c. 1890. About one quarter of the students in this class are African American. The school was located on the East Side at the corner of New York and Smith, which was near the eastern edge of the 5th Ward at the time.
From the collections of the Aurora Historical Society

brought emotion and determination to their efforts that cannot be fully explained in terms of self-interest. What is more, it seems evident that when African Americans did settle in Aurora, they did not find the strident opposition that led to race riots in other cities in the North.

However, they were not openly welcomed either. Aurorans spent a great deal of time pointing out the flaws of the southern lifestyle, the gross injustices of slavery, and post-Reconstruction bigotry and violence. Many sincerely wanted to help African Americans succeed in securing and managing their freedom. Nevertheless, the ghost of racial prejudice often glided through their best efforts. The confusion that these countervailing tendencies of idealism and prejudice produced was left hanging uncomfortably exposed when the idea of free Blacks became the reality of Black neighbors and co-workers. The majority of African Americans in Aurora found themselves excluded from the better-paying jobs and held at arm's length politically. Gradually, subtle racism and an overwhelming sense of condescension hardened into behavioral patterns.

This photo, dated 1894, looks like a 4th of July parade entry. The four young men in the carriage probably would not have been hired to work in the shoe store for which they are advertising— but they could sing.

From the collections of the Aurora Historical Society

A simple advertising slogan on the surface, "We Treat You WHITE," certainly suggests the sense of privilege felt by the racial majority.

From the collections of the Aurora Historical Society

-Chapter 4-
"Unpleasant Glory"

We have seen how local political, religious and social organizations and the press in Aurora all carried ambiguous feelings about African Americans years before the first waves of migrants arrived from the South. There was general support for the notion that slavery was wrong, and that skin color should not impact essential doctrines of justice. Simultaneously, many people in Aurora obviously accepted, without question, the philosophy that African Americans were inferior by nature.

It is not surprising, then, to discover confused and contradictory accounts of the reception encountered by African Americans when they did begin to settle in town. The recollections of people, both White and Black, concerning the arrival of African Americans into the life of Aurora, got entangled in the intertwined lines of idealism and prejudice. The response of Black migrants to this pressure varied with their experiences, their education and their social status.

In the years immediately following emancipation, African Americans had to make an almost unimaginable transition. Born into a system that had taught them to never question or defy any White person, prevented them from having any political voice, and denied them access to education, former slaves suddenly found themselves living among Whites as neighbors, and having to compete with Whites for wage work. As these men and women ran into racist attitudes and behaviors, many naturally resorted to coping strategies that had developed over decades of

From the collections of the Aurora Historical Society

Billy Holland played on one of the earliest baseball teams in Aurora, c. 1890. If surviving evidence is consistent with historical reality, having a black man on the team was unusual. Apparently, athletic skill was more important than skin tone to team manager "Pug" Jungels.

dealing with southern slave culture. One such strategy was to turn the tables, as described through the story-telling tradition of the "Signifying Monkey." In these tales, the sly monkey bests all of the bigger and stronger animals by outwitting them and turning their schemes back on them. The "Brer Rabbit" stories were also based on this idea. Such traditions, molded by the pressures of slavery and post-Reconstruction segregation and then brought out of the South by Black migrants, were nearly incomprehensible to middle-class White Northerners.

Activists and intellectuals of both races agreed that the best means for Blacks to realize their freedom was through education and the democratic process, though some called for change by force and a few promoted a return to Africa. Most African Americans were determined to gain the tools necessary to live freely, as equals with their White neighbors in the South and in the North. They struggled to improve themselves and, with the protection of the Reconstruction policies implemented by Congress in 1866, were making great progress. Reconstruction fell far short of its goals, however, and by 1877 the gains in political, economic and social equality were evaporating in the face of rising violence and discriminatory practices. Confronted with this reversal, Black leaders debated the means to obtain full and unfettered citizenship for all African Americans.

The first to put forward a new approach to the "Negro problem" was Booker T. Washington, founder and principal of the Tuskegee Institute in Alabama. Washington's plan, which he summarized in 1895 during a brief speech that came to be known as the "Atlanta Compromise," focused on economic equality as the immediate goal, with the belief that if African Americans proved themselves necessary within the economy of the United States, political power and civil rights would follow in time.[89] Tuskegee was the embodiment of this philosophy. Black students received agricultural and industrial training so that, through hard work and thrift, they could win the trust of the White majority and earn full citizenship. Naturally, this approach won acclaim among Whites in the South and in the North, since it provided a peaceful means of settling how free Blacks and Whites should live together that did not involve political, social or civil rights. African Americans could be free as long as they were clearly inferior.[90]

While Washington rose quickly to national prominence as the spokesman for his entire race, a competing philosophical approach developed that found its voice in W.E.B. DuBois. Like Washington, DuBois advocated change by improvement and education within the Black community. But he was not content to wait for White America to outgrow assumptions of racial hierarchy, or to gain civil and political rights by slow degrees. DuBois' strategy was to develop political power first by concentrating resources on nurturing and educating those with the intellectual and personal gifts to compete in the arenas of political power; what he famously termed the "Talented Tenth." DuBois believed that a liberal arts education equal to that received by the elite in the White community would enable this top tier to address the problems plaguing African Americans. The Tenth would reinvest their knowledge and skills by developing businesses that would hire Black workers; by teaching and spreading knowledge in the African American community; and by building political influence that would ensure action on the concerns of African Americans.[91]

Like most Whites in the North, Aurorans harbored no doubt that they were a bastion of freedom and civil rights in the United States. And cities like Aurora did hold the promise of vastly improved social conditions. Yet there is evidence of Black Aurorans employing all three of the coping strategies outlined above to deal with various forms of racial discrimination.

As mentioned in Chapter 2, social injustice and even terrible violence did not bring about large-scale migration from the South. Eighty-nine percent of African Americans in the U.S. still lived south of the Mason-Dixon Line in 1910.[92] It was not until individuals and families determined that moving would serve their needs for economic security as well that their desire to move was sparked.

We may never know with certainty what drew the first African American settlers to Aurora. Vague rumors and exaggerated reports of the economic possibilities of northern Illinois, such as drew the Lake brothers from Ohio, were likely also circulating in Virginia and Tennessee. Perhaps stories about Aurora's prosperity and outspoken Republican politics aroused the desire among those first few to try beginning a new life. Maybe they were on their way to Chicago, and discovered Aurora by accident.

Once they arrived, the first concern of all immigrants, regardless of race, was to secure employment. Isaiah "Ike" Carter, whose family arrived in Aurora in the mid-to-late 1870s, alluded to this when asked what had drawn them. He responded by saying that his grandmother, Catherine Cattlet, was acting on reports of employment opportunities in Aurora. Carter said Cattlet found working conditions "were not too good, but enough for poor people to start."[93]

Bennett and Susan Carter Family, c. 1896. Identifications based on 1900 Census.

Pearl, Susan, Shuster, Bennett
Isaiah, Ollie, Cornelius
Blanche, Lute
Bennett

Copied with permission from the collection of Teri Parker

European immigrants began to dominate the labor market in Aurora by 1860. Industrial work and skilled positions, in particular, were rarely available to African Americans when they first began arriving in Aurora between 1860 and 1870. For confirmation of this, one need only look at the occupations listed in the census reports. Most African Americans worked in positions of menial labor or as private or public servants. Moreover, a series of seemingly unrelated articles that appeared in the Beacon early in 1864 raise the possibility that White workers were preferred.

At the time, the country was debating the best means to assist the recently freed slaves. Thousands of African Americans, termed "contraband of war" by the Union Army, were living a harsh existence in camps with insufficient supplies. On February 25 and again on March 3, the Beacon ran articles discussing options for aiding Black refugees in camps along the southern stretches of the Mississippi River. In the first, the author proposed that "it is our duty to accept the facts of destitution and disorganization among the freedmen, and begin at once to reform the reform. To make the slave free is not enough; we must give him the opportunity to see his freedom, and, when necessary, must teach him to use it."[94] The following week, a report from the New York Post was reprinted locally that asserted "No reasoning is needed to show that a day's work well done is worth as much to an employer when performed by Black arms as if the laborer had the fairest complexion in the world."[95] Yet the Beacon published the following editorial just one week later:

> *The present and prospective high prices of farm products are stimulating the farmers to plant and sow all that can be cultivated and harvested. The war has told fearfully on the*

population of the country, and the question of farm help has become a grave one. There are but two ways to obviate the difficulties arising from its scarcity. The introduction of labor saving machinery and the employment of the foreign population now in vast numbers landing upon our shore. Last year there arrived in New York alone nearly 160,000 emigrants. These men, though ignorant of methods of farming in this country, soon learn sufficient to make them of great value to employers and answer tolerably well to fill the vacant places.[96]

The articles from the previous two weeks certainly seem to contradict the idea that the only two solutions to the farm labor crisis were the introduction of machines and the importation of European men "ignorant of methods of farming in this country." When it came to recruiting workers into Aurora, there seems to be a gap between the stated belief in equality and actual practice. Why did the editor ignore this large labor pool, many of whom had some direct agricultural experience, in favor of White European immigrants? Were there political or logistical blocks to getting African American workers out of the South? There were no follow-up reports to confirm how farmers dealt with this critical labor shortage.

If African Americans were arriving in Aurora with hopes of utilizing their skills in trades and professions, they soon discovered that there were a variety of obstacles to overcome. The most obvious was simply the lack of offers. Employers in cities across the North were reluctant to hire Black applicants. Usually, their reasoning was based on preconceived ideas about Black and White workers. Primarily, employers complained that Black employees were inexperienced. In addition, managers believed that African Americans could not be depended upon because they had a roving nature, and were easily tempted to move.⁹⁷ As with most stereotypes, a kernel of truth was expanded to typify the entire racial group. Many of the early African American migrants moving to northern cities lacked industrial skills, and were unprepared for the realities of urban life and industrial work. However, many European immigrant groups, and rural immigrants generally, had similar problems. Still, these issues of transition were added to the body of "evidence" in building a case of racial inferiority.⁹⁸ Furthermore, employers worried that White workers would refuse to share skilled labor. As one author put it, "Employers seek harmony in their labor force, and harmony rarely followed the promotion of Negro workers to positions of authority over Caucasians."⁹⁹

On the other hand, many employers took a paternalistic attitude that was demeaning, but at least offered hope of jobs. These men found great promise in African American workers. According to one survey, employers listed the following benefits of Black laborers:¹⁰⁰

1) They are loyal to employers

2) They take a proprietary interest in the business

3) They do not strike, or become easily enflamed against employers

4) They are easily controlled and worked

5) Those least suited to the work are the first to quit, easing manager's job

African Americans who managed to find ways into semi-skilled and skilled positions, as well as individuals who attempted to circumvent the system by working on their own, were typically frustrated to find the trades unions standing in their way. The antipathy that the unions demonstrated toward Black workers, in spite of common interests, is well documented. Unions complained bitterly that employers used African American workers to lower the bar on wages, and employed them as strike breakers. However, when African Americans approached the unions, hoping to join and thereby increase the pressure to improve wages and working conditions for everyone, they found the doors closed. Eventually, like a self-fulfilling prophecy, frustrated Black workers chose to fend for themselves rather than continue asking for admittance, at which point the unions' worst fears were realized.[101]

Some unions had race restrictive provisions written into their charters. More often, locals simply looked for subtle and expedient ways to exclude Black applicants. In commenting on his research into twenty-one unions in Buffalo, NY, one researcher noted "Some are quite frank in admitting that they can easily find some excuse to prevent the admission of Negro workmen."[102]

Isaiah "Ike" Carter, an African American born in Aurora in 1886, had first hand experience with exclusion from the local unions. He was a plasterer by profession, having learned that trade from his father, Ben. "I got quite a reputation," Carter recounted in an oral interview conducted by the Aurora Historical Society in 1988. "I went out contracting a year later, when I was older."[103]

The subject of labor unions seemed to be troubling to Carter, as the following exchange illustrates.

Carter: *They wouldn't take me in the union 'cause I had too much speed. They didn't want that because then the others have to follow suit, see. I applied for the union two or three times.*

Sarna: *Was there any difficulty getting into the union because you were Black, do you feel like. . .?*

Carter: *No, that wasn't the question. The question with me was speed. I was too fast. If I got in there they'd have to compete. They didn't want that. Well, I didn't blame 'em for it.*

Ike Carter trained with his father, and continued his father's path toward economic independence and a solid middle class life for himself and his family.

Copied with permission from the collection of Teri Parker

Sarna: *You eventually got in, right?*

Carter: *No, no. I contracted for myself. I had all the business I could handle, maybe more.*[104]

Every time the interviewer raised the subject of race, Carter steadfastly refused to admit that his race had impeded his career. Instead, he stressed his success in business.

Carter: *The big folks in the Caucasian race, like the Heitkotters and them folks. . .well Heitkotter had the advantage because he was German, you see. And he came in, and the Germans got behind him and pushed him right up.*

Sarna: *So it was difficult being a Black businessman trying to compete against a lot of the White businesses?*

Carter: *No, not too much.*[105]

Carter did not mean to say that his business was made harder by racism, although that was the way it sounded to the interviewer. Rather, he was pointing out that the large population of German immigrants rather naturally supported a German plasterer. Whether those German customers would have hired a Black contractor, even if no German alternative had been available, is another question entirely. According to Carter, that was not the issue.

However, his exclusion from the union haunted the conversation. Note the subtle change in Carter's tone when he brings the subject up himself later. The focus of the story is still his own ability and success, but there is a hint that his work had to be superior, to overcome the union's unwillingness to allow him access to their influence. The reason for the union's obstinacy is also more vague than the previous excuse of work speed.

> *I had a fellow named Mike Smith; he was of the League of Plasterers. I come to him as my sponsor. At the union meetin', every time I go down there when they had the votes for me, he'd get about half drunk and they wouldn't take his word. They'd go meetin' after meetin', same thing. And one day I got so mad, I said 'I can plaster good enough to [inaudible].' So I said 'I'm going out by myself.' Well, I started out to advertise for my business. And I got so much work I couldn't take care of it. Every job takes care of itself. 'Who done that?' 'Ike Carter done that.' 'Oh! I'll go get him.'*[106]

Despite his unwillingness to openly say that racism had kept him out of the union, or disadvantaged him in securing new business, Carter could not have been blind to the contradictions in his situation. Perhaps he hesitated to tell the young White man conducting the interview what he really felt was going on. Maybe he felt that dwelling on what others did only distracted from what he wanted people to remember: his skill in his profession, and his success in running his own business. Whatever the reason, he opted not to discuss race in straightforward terms.

One of the few professions considered quite open to African American men in the late nineteenth century was that of barber. There were a number of barbers among the wave of migrants who arrived shortly after the Civil War. Some worked in shops owned by White men. Several owned and operated their own establishments.

Those who owned their own shops found a market niche among the youth of Aurora. Decades later, several contributors to the Now and Then column in the Beacon-News commented on these shops, and recalled with fondness their first shave at the hands of such men as Mose Webb and John Smith. Each one openly admitted that the African American barbers got their first business because, as one put it, "a youth

Looking east at the intersection of Main Street (now Galena) and LaSalle, 1886. Mose Webb gradually moved from operating a barber shop with candy for sale to opening a confectionery. His candy store was in the small building with the peaked roof near the center of this photo.

From the collections of the Aurora Historical Society

with his first growth of fuzz hesitates to go into a big three or four chair shop and be kidded."[107] Yet if pubescent embarrassment prompted the first visit to the smaller shops, off the main thoroughfares, the kindly treatment the boys received made them regular customers. One former customer remembered:

> *I wanted a shave, but hesitated to go to a regular white man's shop and be 'kidded,' so I went to John Smith and he was very serious about it—and never laughed. John held my trade until my fuzz grew to man's strength.*[108]

The flip side of the process that brought the boys to these barbers was the acknowledged need to leave once the boys were ready to move into the realm of the "regular White men." There is no question that the sole reason this man broke off his association with Smith was race. It was acceptable for young boys to socialize with their African American neighbors. But clearly, such a relationship was considered a phase to be outgrown, like the embarrassing peach fuzz beard.

African American barbers took advantage of their position, such as it was. They catered to boys in their teens and younger. Half of Mose Webb's one chair barber shop was filled with candy. He sold "'twofer' cigars, stogies and cheroots, fine cut and plug tobacco. Also, he sold tops and marbles."[109]

As large numbers of African Americans settled in Aurora, they created a variety of political, religious and social organizations to attend to the needs of the community. The first were churches. On 13 June 1862, seven "faithful Christian workers" formed the first Black congregation, a Methodist mission that the Annual Conference attached to the Mendota Circuit. This group met initially in a small room over Pierpont and Wright's grocery, at 18 Main Street. In 1867, a group of

The congregation of the Main Street Baptist Church gathered outside of their building, c. 1905.

Copied with permission from the collection of Main Street Baptist Church

African Americans who had been worshipping with the predominantly White congregation of the Park Place Baptist Church elected to leave and form their own church under the leadership of Reverend Barnett. Reverend Buttons, the pastor of Park Place, assisted the budding new congregation.[111]

Few specifics are known about the activities that went on in and around the churches, aside from worship services and Sunday schools. On New Years Day, 1873, with Aurora suffering through a winter in which temperatures reached -33°, a report appeared in the Beacon from the Ladies' Christian Union, which read in part:

> *There is, perhaps, just now a greater amount of suffering among the colored people than the white. Both colored churches extend all the assistance in their power, but their membership is small, their financial resources limited, and the burden proves much greater than they can carry.*[112]

It is likely that, in addition to the usual social and religious outreach common to most churches regardless of denomination, these African American congregations also functioned as community centers; places where people could gather and socialize, hold meetings and provide entertainment. In many cities, when African Americans found themselves shut out of public parks, restaurants, clubs and theatres, they turned to their churches.[113] The following item, which ran in the Beacon, demonstrates that churches in Aurora did serve in this capacity sometimes.

> *The colored people, under the direction of Mrs. Robbins, give another of their enjoyable concerts on Tuesday evening next, at the African M. E. Church, Benton Street, the programme consisting mainly of plantation songs. The price of admission is placed at the low sum of fifteen cents, and it is hoped that the vocalists will be greeted by a full house.*[114]

Also, as we saw happen with several of the local Protestant churches in previous chapters, the intersection of social concern with religious fervor often created community action groups. Some time around 1868, a group was formed in Aurora under the name Right of Suffrage League. Although there is no evidence indicating direct ties to the African Methodist Episcopal Church, the group did meet in the same location, as mentioned in Aurora's First Annual Directory:

> *The colored men of the city of Aurora have established a Society, with the above title, numbering now near twenty members. The objects are: First, to use their best endeavors eventually to obtain the right of suffrage; secondly, to prepare for the care of each other should sickness or trouble overtake them. They hold weekly meetings, in rooms over Pierpont & Wright's store. The officers are: Moses Webb, President; Charles Steele, Vice President; Wm. Rogers, Secretary.*[115]

The formation of all Black churches and political organizations was a critical step toward independence for African Americans in Aurora. The men and women who founded these bodies wanted to prove that they were prepared to provide the needs and wants of their own community, just as the Germans, Swedes and Luxembourgers were doing. Soon after, social groups appeared, to provide the cultural bond and strengthen community ties.

In 1873, the Beacon noted that African Americans from the community were planning an event with deep emotional and cultural significance.

> *The colored people of this vicinity have their Emancipation Celebration this year at Elgin, on the 1st of August.*[116]

The brevity of this announcement makes identifying the purpose of this group difficult. Was this celebration political in nature, with political and patriotic speeches, like Independence Day? Perhaps it was more like New Year's Eve, social in nature, an opportunity for African Americans from the surrounding area to get together and have a party. We cannot even be certain that "colored people" was as universal as it sounds. Was the party an open invitation to all Black people living in the region? The only thing that is clear from this item is that African Americans in Aurora and Elgin, and possibly other towns along the Fox River Valley, were networking beyond the confines of their respective hometowns. Sadly, the <u>Beacon</u> followed up the following week only with a terse statement confirming the event. No newspaper accounts from Elgin survive to shed further light on the observance of this holiday that was so important for Black Americans locally, regionally, and nationally.

Ten years later, the following announcement ran:

> *The colored people of Kane and Kendall counties are forming an Emancipation Society, and are to hold their initial meeting at Batavia this week. It will have in charge all celebrations, and matters generally concerning the interests of the colored people of these counties.*[117]

If the celebration did not have a political agenda before, it sounds as though one had developed. And in the tradition of the previous festival, the organization formalized the regional network. African Americans were looking to build a support base, perhaps with an eye toward consolidating some political power.

On 19 October 1872, well before the above notices about the Emancipation Society, a small but important announcement ran in the <u>Beacon</u> that spoke of significant developments in African American society locally.

> *A lodge of colored Free Masons has been organized in this city, styled the "Keystone Lodge." The following are the*

officers elected: John Collins, W. M.; Calvin Bogert, S. W.; John Hall, J. W.; Moses Webb, S. D.; J. Jackson, J. D.; Clark Thomasson and James Stewart, Stewards; M. DeCoursey, Tyler; E. Coleman, Treasurer; W. J. Isham, Secretary.[118]

There are several reasons why the formation of a Masonic Lodge for African Americans was important. First, it provided another social outlet beyond the church walls. Freemasonry allowed "the socially ambitious to join an exclusive society."[119] There were dances, dinners and occasions at which members of Aurora's Lodge could mix and mingle. And it provided a network of other lodges, expanding the sense of community beyond the city limits, as the following news item proves.

The Keystone Lodge of colored Masons celebrated the New Year by a dance at the City Hall which was well attended, and all present—among whom were many from Batavia and Chicago—seemed to be enjoying themselves intensely when we dropped in upon them about midnight. The Keystone Lodge was organized October 16th, 1872, is running in handsome shape, and with the reputation of this their first party, they will have little difficulty hereafter in filling their hall for a dance. The Lodge meets in the hall over Mix and Miller's Bank, and the proceeds of this dance will contribute to furnishing the same.[120]

Secondly, the effort to bring African Americans under the wing of Freemasonry was largely political. Prince Hall, who founded the first Masonic Lodge for Black men, hoped that the Mason's message of unity and brotherhood for all men would be colorblind. It was his hope that Freemasonry, with its wide and powerful connections across the nation and around the globe, could be a means for African Americans to integrate into free society.[121] Unfortunately, the genesis of the Keystone Lodge did not represent a leap forward in race relations in Aurora. As with most of American society, Masonry ascribed to the custom of "separate but equal." Lodge 15 was entirely segregated from the other lodges in town, who did not acknowledge African American Masons in any official capacity. The other Masonic organizations met in a building on Stolp Island, while this small group of Black men established their Hall in rooms over Mix and Miller's Bank on River Street in the West Side. Nevertheless, the Keystone Lodge did raise the visibility of African Americans in Aurora. At the very least, the previous announcements show that the local press was reporting their burgeoning success.

Finally, even though it was segregated from the other lodges, there was some resonance and recognition of common purpose. That common purpose was service. The members of the Keystone Lodge, like all Masons, took on the duty of community service. They were tradesmen and businessmen, and at least a few could be considered middle-class. Calvin Boger was a well-known mason and independent contractor. Edmund Coleman was listed in the 1870 City Directory as a stone cutter. According to James McNeil, the Worshipful Master of the Keystone Lodge in 1999, one of the founding members was a blacksmith and farrier.[122] Mose Webb and Milton DeCoursey both owned barbershops. These men contributed their time, talents and resources to assisting their neighbors. Obviously, this had great impact on African Americans, who were very often the people in Aurora most in need of assistance. But beyond the observable "good deeds," the existence of this organization made clear to everyone, Black and White, that African Americans were both willing and able to take the active role in managing their own affairs.[123] Furthermore, it was a clear indication of their desire to be recognized as community minded in the broadest terms.

Around the turn of the century, African Americans formed a chapter of the Knights of Pythias in Aurora. Much of what was discussed above probably holds true for this organization as well, although little information is available. Compare the article above, about the Masons New Year's Eve party, with the following:

> *Aurora colored Knights of Pythias will go to Rockford Sunday to observe the annual celebration with Forest City lodge, No. 41. They will be joined by Elgin, who will go with special cars . . .. The Reverend Boyd, former pastor of Aurora African Methodist church, will preach the sermon. A special car will leave Aurora at 7:30 o'clock for Elgin, the trip to be made by trolley to Rockford over the Belvidere line.*[124]

To begin with, both of these reports concern public events of private, exclusive clubs. This shows some recognition of an increasingly visible Black community by the White community. At the very least, those who read the paper were aware that African American branch groups of the Masons and the Knights of Pythias existed. Additionally, the appearance of these announcements suggests that some African Americans read the local paper. Why else would these clubs cultivate a relationship with the Beacon, or submit a press release for an event of concern only to members? Finally, both of the events in question were regional, rather than local. Black residents of Aurora were looking beyond their city borders in search of what sociologist Milton Gordon called "primary" relationships. According to Gordon, two people of the same social class, but of different ethnic groups, will probably share similarities in behavior, attitudes and beliefs, but they will not have a sense of "peoplehood." Conversely, two people of the same ethnic background, but occupying different social strata, will share a sense of peoplehood, but not behavioral similarities. Only when both conditions are met do you have a primary relationship, or what sociologist Franklin Giddings called "consciousness of kind." Primary relationships are important, because it is really only in that context that people can truly relax and interact easily and honestly.[125]

Rising class-consciousness also manifested itself demographically. According to local historian Susan Palmer, by 1880 "Aurorans increasingly sorted themselves out according to socioeconomic status in their choice of residential neighborhoods."[126] The census figures seem to bear this view out for the African American community. As noted earlier, the 1880 Census shows that, while most of the Black population was concentrated in the southern wards, a number of families moved into neighborhoods further north and east, away from the downtown and the river. While certainly not areas of great wealth, these were respectable areas with good homes. They were also, for the most part, areas where the White working-class and middle-class lived.

It is telling that the areas White Aurorans seemed to remember most as Black enclaves were poor districts. Several contributors to the *Now and Then* column in the Beacon, in thinking back to their youth, remembered two buildings, both of which were referred to as the "barracks." These decrepit frame buildings were apparently tenements "in which colored people and also white people lived."[127]

Lloyd Ochsenschlager vividly recalled the back alleys behind his parents' grocery shop because, as a boy, he and his friends played "in the rear of our store, along the single track railroad." He continued:

> *It was a curious little community back there. When the stores of brick and stone were built on Main Street and Broadway, the original little old pioneer frame stores were moved back there, along the tracks, placed with no regularity. In one of them Octave Landry, captain of the old*

This building stood near the corner of Lake and Holbrook (now Benton). A contributor to the *Now and Then* column referred to it as "The Barracks." Other contributors used "The Barracks" to refer to at least one other building that stood on Stolp Island.

From the collections of the Aurora Historical Society

The house in the foreground stood behind the Cotton Mills on the west end of New York Street Bridge, near the current YWCA. Writing on the back of this photo indicates that the house was occupied by African Americans, though they were not named.

From the collections of the Aurora Historical Society

> 'Mayflower' boat, had his carpenter shop; and in another lived the well known colored family of Meadows; and in another was the Barlow family with 'Nick' and 'Yatzie,' two well known town characters.[128]

The boys in the Meadows family were among his nearest neighbors, and they became his friends and playmates. "These colored boys," he adds, "were very popular around town; all keen and bright lads, and quite accomplished. They could sing and dance, and fight some; and were just full of fun."[129]

Ochsenschlager's summary of their talents is a worthy list of boyish traits. However, his memory of the boys' father, as we shall see later, is little different, leaving one to wonder whether these playmates were allowed to outgrow their boyish charm.

As African Americans settled into formerly all-White neighborhoods, the amount of interracial contact necessarily increased. "Ike" Carter, whose family lived at New York and Union on the East Side, remembered playing baseball and hide-and-seek with neighbor kids who were French, Swedish, Norwegian and Irish, but "not too many colored people." At Brady School, where he attended through the eighth grade, "there were quite a few [African Americans] there." When asked how the White and Black children got along, Carter downplayed any trouble. Still, his answer betrays some serious problems.

> Of course there was name calling at one time or the other. Sometimes they'd even fight, and if they were Black they'd get beaten. But I didn't have much contact with that stuff. Not too much fightin' goin' on at all.[130]

The stories of White and Black children playing together, and the kindly memories of by-gone days spent hanging out in African American owned shops, suggest that the White youth of Aurora had reasonably

Historically, the area known as Pigeon Hill had few African American residents. In 1890, when this photo was taken, Eddie Harding (back row) was apparently the only black student in his Brady School class.

From the collections of the Aurora Historical Society

good relations with African Americans in the community. However, little extant material demonstrates a similar relationship on the part of the adult population. The wistful memories of men who treated shy boys with dignity, the fondness for neighborhood friends who were admired for their ability to fight, and other tokens of respect disappear with age. They are replaced with sly digs, mean jokes and an air of superiority.

Jim Meadows, in particular, was widely remembered in the Now and Then columns as a source of continuous "fun," generally in the form of pranks at his expense. In Lloyd Ochsenschlager's words, Meadows was "a good natured clown" and "a butt of many jokes and hero of numerous stories." Though he was well known in town, nobody in the White community seemed to care much about the man. Only one small advertisement, in hundreds of issues of the Beacon, gave any indication as to Meadow's profession.

> *James Meadows City Laundry, on Water Street, in rear of Fitch House, just south of Roach's livery stable, gives prompt and careful attention to all orders for washing and ironing. Be sure to call upon James.*[131]

All of the stories about Meadows seem to revolve around his willingness to participate in schemes and jokes hatched by young White men in town to either embarrass him, or use him to embarrass others. The mean spiritedness of many of the stories is quite stark. In a classic example of the East-West rivalry, a men's shop on the West Side introduced a new fashion trend into Aurora; a white derby with a black band. These hats became all the rage. The competitors on the East Side had none in stock, and were unable to compete. One of the East Side shop owners, in order to kill interest in the fad, bought one of the hats and gave it to Jim Meadows, on the condition that he "parade the business streets all one day, wearing the same, and an advertisement on his back calling attention to it." "Needless to say," concluded the author, "the local vogue for white derbies was nipped in the bud."[132] In a separate incident, a group of young men from the Idle Hour Club did their traditional New Year's social calls in a home-made sleigh, with Meadows dressed in livery as footman for their "coach" providing the crowning touch to their comical creation.

Meadows was not the only African American caricatured as a fool. "Lutz" White memorialized Ben Mason, who worked as a boot-black in front of the C. B. & Q. station, in two stories. In the first story, Mason fell in behind a parade of Aurora's military drill team known as the Light Guard, strutting along and hamming for the crowd. An African American woman referred to as "Aunty" Triggs (see photo on page 36) called out to Mason, telling him to quit fooling around and disgracing his emancipation. In the second story, a local police officer decided to play a joke on young Mason, with the help of three of the "Windsor Club boys." The policeman and his cohorts confronted the boot-black, who was wearing jeans and a sleeveless T-shirt, and authoritatively informed him that he needed to find more suitable attire. They told Mason that he was the first impression that visitors had of the town, and that he needed to be more aware of his important position. As White told the story, Mason was sufficiently awed by the delegation to put together an effort that proved comical in its creation; a bright red and black seersucker coat, a pink and white dickey, paper collar, straw hat and polished shoes.[133]

In light of the one-sided nature of the source material for these stories, it is helpful to consider that these stories may have deeper

The author believes that the man standing on the back of the "sleigh" is Jim Meadows, and that this photograph shows members of the Idle Hour Club making New Year's calls as described in the Aurora Evening Post, 28 November 1894.

From the collections of the Aurora Historical Society

significance. Who was taking advantage of whom? Did Meadows agree to be a part of such schemes because he felt compelled to do so, or was he using the opportunity presented to take a poke at a man otherwise out of his reach? Could Mason have been playing tricks on the authority figures in these stories, in the tradition of the "Signifying Monkey" fables? What White described as Mason's "convulsing buffoonery" could easily be a mocking of the Light Guard and their proud display. And it does not take much imagination to see the outrageous costume Mason prepared in the second story as sly retribution on the four White men, by playing the stereotype out to its ludicrous extreme. Of course this is speculation, but it is not an unreasonable hypothesis.

Take the idea another step. The coverage in the <u>Beacon</u> of the Independence Day celebrations of 1876, commemorating the nation's centennial, may be highlighting a rising conflict in racial attitudes in Aurora. According to the newspaper's account of the enormous parade that launched the day's affairs, African American participation was limited to a single entry: a car, drawn by thirteen white horses to represent the thirteen original states, and each horse led by a "colored groom."[134]

At the conclusion of the parade, Reverend William A. Bartlett of Chicago gave a speech, a portion of which he devoted to the need for racial understanding.

> I was going to say that there are some great questions yet to be solved. There is the race question. We have not settled that yet. Our constitutions and laws declare the equality of all men before the law, and yet we fight the principle to the bitter end. How long it was, and how much blood and treasure had been shed before we were willing to make the negro even free. Yet the first blood poured out in the Revolution was that of Crispus Attucks, a mulatto, who was

shot down by British soldiery in the streets of Boston. That blood has cried from the earth til the shackles were stricken from every negro slave. But it yet remains for us to help the members of that despised race fairly on their feet, and electrify them with the magnetism of popular education. [Applause][135]

This speech failed utterly to address the inequities in employment opportunities, the lack of direct representation in local politics, or other issues that African Americans in Aurora might have recognized as important to solving the "race question" for their town. Reverend Bartlett, like many Northerners, could see no trouble any closer than Dixie.

Immediately following Bartlett's speech was a burlesqued version of the morning's parade, which a reporter for the <u>Beacon</u> detailed with relish. In this parade, African American men were the stars, mocking the day's biggest event. Martin Long was appointed marshal of the "Calathumpian" parade, and carried an enormous sword. Jim Meadows took the position of "poet." Pete LaMar represented the Goddess of Liberty.

This second parade, like the "clowning" of Ben Mason mentioned above, may well be an example of African Americans taking advantage of an opportunity to "send up" the dominant culture. The predominantly White crowd, represented by the reporter, saw only Black men cutting up. Was there more to it for the participants? Were Long, Meadows and LaMar subtly responding to the fact that the only African Americans participating in the first parade did so as servants? Nothing in the newspaper reports indicates that anyone in the White community saw any irony in the alignment of these three events. In fact, three White men, calling themselves "Three Happy Mokes," participated in the

This entry in the 1913 4th of July Calathumpian Parade was intended to shame the C.B.&Q. into replacing the train station, which locals viewed as unworthy of Aurora's size and stature. Is the addition of the black paperboy meant to deepen the sense of a poor first impression, reminiscent of the Windsor Club prank about Ben Mason's appearance?

From the collections of the Aurora Historical Society

second parade in blackface. The blackface act won the First Prize for the day, another irony that went without comment.[136]

As the years passed, prejudice in Aurora grew increasingly open. Residents of the town that had so vehemently opposed slavery turned out in droves to see "Terry and Stecher's Congo Slave Troupe of Minstrels," or to hear the local "colored people . . . give another of their enjoyable concerts . . . of plantation songs."[137] The myth of the "happy darkie" that southern plantation owners had tried to use to stave off the abolitionists was now popular culture, and it created an insidious cycle of racism. Whites across the country expected all Blacks to be the lazy, fun loving fools portrayed in minstrel shows. Of course, such behaviors preclude one from success in a capitalistic, market economy where ruthlessness and daring are admired. In other words, White society demanded behavior that insured that Blacks would falter in the arenas of power, and then placed the blame for their failure on deficiency of character.[138] Moreover, rejecting the role of "good natured clown" often led to being labeled "uppity," and to other more severe forms of backlash.

At the same time, the press in Aurora was marginalizing African Americans. As the nineteenth century drew to a close, articles, social announcements, even advertisements relating to African American businesses, appear less frequently in the newspaper. If the annual Emancipation Celebration took place again after 1883, the Beacon did not report it. The only event involving an African American that did make the paper in 1890 was a lecture, given by "Aunty" Triggs in the public hall over the city court room. "She took for her text 'Coming to the Front,' and was listened to by a medium sized audience."[139] It would

West High students wearing blackface stage a minstrel show in the school auditorium, c. 1915.

From the collections of the Aurora Historical Society

be interesting to know the racial makeup of that audience, but that was not recorded.

When the escalating tensions in Europe that had brought record numbers of immigrants to the United States broke into open warfare, many African Americans seized the opportunities that were presented. As the labor market loosened up men and women, many of whom were skilled in trades, finally got the chance to work in meaningful positions for reasonable compensation. The United States' entry into World War I gave them further opportunity to demonstrate their newfound sense of value to the system. For many Black men, service in the armed forces was more than patriotic duty; it was another chance to break down the barriers between themselves and the rest of society.

Henry Boger was one of those young men. A former football star for East High, Boger went on to attend Oberlin and the University of Illinois, earning his degree in education. When the U. S. entered the war, he gave up his teaching job to enlist in the Army. He attended officer training at a camp for African Americans, and went to France with a lieutenant's commission in command of an all-Black company. Boger found France an education unlike anything he had yet experienced.

> *The people everywhere have received us with open arms, and have made us feel like we are men, not half men as our U. S. whites do. We wine and dine at the best with the best and get along fine, except where the U. S. white is he has brought his ways with him here.*[141]

The frustration expressed in this exchange implies that Boger had some experience with being treated as a "half man." He did not say that his life in Aurora contributed to that frustration, but the universality of the remark certainly carries implications. The assumed recognition and agreement in the statements to his mother mean that he took for granted that she would understand to what he referred, regardless of where individual events may have taken place. Racism was so endemic it did not need specific mention.

Boger's unit was literally "in the trenches." A great deal of anger is evident in some of the letters Boger wrote to his family. In one, he expressed the belief that his company had been sent back to the front after only a day or two of rest, to give early relief to White soldiers. And in the following excerpt, a playful lament for Black nurses suddenly becomes a racial clarion call:

> *You people at home are not doing your bit, are you. It is awful to wake up and look into the face of a white nurse. They are very kind, but oh how one would feel to see a brown skin. Our slogan is take no prisoners, so I say to you give the American white man no mercy, he is crooked, and when death comes, you can smile and say I played my part.*[142]

Boger was clearly not fighting this war to preserve the American way of life as he had known it. He may have joined believing that the fight to make the world safe for democracy included securing that right to himself in his hometown.

Many of the African Americans who fought overseas in World War I came home dissatisfied with the status quo. At the same time, those who had moved from the South into northern urban centers had found prosperity they had never known, and were unwilling to let it go simply because White soldiers were returning. The National Association for the Advancement of Colored People and the National Urban League saw quick and enormous growth in membership, as

Henry Boger, probably during training at Fort Des Moines.

Calvin Boger poses for a quick portrait, c. 1915.

Reprinted with permission from the collection of Jeanne Boger Jones

returning veterans and the new urbanized African American moved into active political life. His letters suggest that, had he lived, Henry Boger would have been one of those who chose an active political path. Sadly, Lieutenant Boger was killed in the closing days of the war.

The two brief accounts of the life of Calvin Boger that follow exemplify the racial gulf that was widening in Aurora. Calvin Boger, Henry's father, was very well known around town, in both the White and Black communities. What is interesting to note, though, is how he was remembered. The accounts are given in the order published. The first is the obituary as published in the <u>Beacon</u>.

> *Calvin T. Boger, 81, one of the best known colored men in this section of the country, died at his home 228 Claim Street, this morning at 2:15 o'clock after a lingering illness. He had been a resident of Aurora for about 60 years, coming here after the Civil War, in which he fought as a member of the Union Army.*
>
> *The deceased was born at Hickory Flats, Ga. in 1844 and spent his boyhood days in slavery. At the outbreak of the Civil War he ran away and joined the command of Captain Hattery, an Aurora man. He fought through the war with the cavalry and was wounded twice.*
>
> *After the war he came to Aurora and went to work in the Hattery bakery. Later he became a mason and bricklayer contractor and put up some of the first brick buildings in Aurora, among them being the Frazier factory. He took a prominent part in Republican politics for years and held several positions at the state house in Springfield. He was the second colored man to arrive in Aurora after the war.*[143]

Now compare that with an account written some years later by "Lutz" White, as a historical remembrance in *Now and Then*.

He (Boger) was Aurora's fourth colored pioneer; a youth with a credible war record, whose stock in trade was health, strength, a happy disposition, a faculty of making friends, and an heritage of common sense and good judgement.

The subject of our story was born in bondage on a plantation in a territory known at that time as "Hickory Flats," not far from Atlanta, Ga. He was one of 13 children who went by the name of McDonough, after the master.

At the age of 12 years, just previous to the breaking out of the war Calvin ran away, to make his way to the northern land of freedom. As all refugees did at that time, he changed his name to conceal his identity and adopted that of "Boger."

When the war broke out "Cal" found himself within the Union lines, just a boy with no particular destination and with nothing to do but follow the army.

In his wanderings he met with two different officers, who were to have an important influence on his future life-- Dr. Abner Hard and Captain Hattery, both from Aurora. The former was regimental surgeon of the 8th Illinois cavalry, and as the story goes, "Cal," a bright lad of 13 years, was unofficially appointed orderly or personal attendant of Dr. Hard. He had also been with Captain Hattery and others in the same capacity.

While he served his country faithfully during the war he was never enlisted officially, on which account he was not eligible to membership in the G. A. R.

After the war Cal Boger came to Aurora a lad of 17 years. To the best recollection of the family today, he was brought to Aurora by Captain Hattery as an attendant, and henceforth made this his home.

"Cal's" first job was in the Hattery bakery, where he was a faithful worker. He left there, however, to accept a position as cook in the old Huntoon hotel.

In his youth he attended Sunday school at First Congregational, the historic "church of abolition." At this time the Congregationalists were active in establishing the colored people and guiding them in their new life of freedom.

Later "Cal" hired out as mason tender with "Put" Howard, one time mayor of Aurora, and by close application

> *soon learned the trade and launched in business for himself. From that time until his death "Cal" was a well-known figure in Aurora.*
>
> *Ask any old time citizen or business man and he will tell you "Cal" Boger was reliable; a man of honor, integrity and morals. He was a home loving man and reared a family of eight children. He was never active in politics or religion, altho his family were leaders in the A. M. E. church.*
>
> *As a contractor Mr. Boger did mostly residential work and repair contracts. He also specialized on installation of brick furnaces and cisterns. He built the first brick church of the colored Methodists; and erected the first city water tower*[144]

To begin with, there are some important discrepancies to deal with in these accounts of Calvin Boger's life. The first glaring difference is his war record. In the obituary, he was a soldier with the cavalry. This does not seem likely, and sounds like a story that got embellished over time. According to White, Boger was an attendant, implying little more than a servant's role. What he did do during those years with the army is not known, but no mention of Calvin Boger was made in the written histories of the units of either Captain Hattery or Dr. Hard.[145] Calvin Boger's granddaughter, Jeanne Jones, believes that White's story is accurate.[146]

In a similar contradiction, White declared that Boger was not interested in politics while the obituary claims he was an active Republican who held state offices. It could be that Boger's political activities waned over time. The Illinois "Blue Book," which lists state office holders, did not record Boger in any position, nor is there any indication that he held office locally. This set of contradictions, unfortunately, remains unresolved. The evidence seems to support

White's version. Still, White's outright denial of any political activity seems out of place. Why even mention it?

Finally, a subtler point of contention arises when comparing the writing styles of these two memorials. Obviously, the authors had different purposes for writing and different constraints, which partly explains the different styles. But look closely at the verbs each employed. In the first account, Boger was the actor. He ran away and joined the army; he came to Aurora; he went to work in the Hattery Bakery; he became a mason. In White's version of Boger's life, many of the most important events were arranged through the beneficence of White men. His summary of Boger's talents seems to be that he was a good worker, he was easy to get along with, and he did not rock the boat.

Susan Palmer, in assessing the differences between immigrant experiences in a small city like Aurora as compared with Chicago, reasoned that integration may have been more rapid and less traumatic in the smaller setting. In her words, "Because ethnic groups were considerably smaller, it was less likely that they could remain insulated from the rest of society." The larger metropolitan area was more attractive to those in search of "a quick fortune and some high adventure," as well as people "who wanted to make their living strictly within the ethnic community." These options were not available in the small urban setting. But a city like Aurora could offer a safer, more stable community.[147]

In many regards, this assessment coincides with what occurred within the African American community as well. The economic opportunities were far more limited in Aurora than they were in Chicago at the end of the nineteenth and the beginning of the twentieth century.

Doubtless, many people dissatisfied with the pace of improvement in Aurora were drawn to Chicago and Detroit. However, the majority of African Americans moving into Aurora between 1860 and 1920 arrived |in family units. The neighborhoods of houses, rather than blocks of apartments and the smaller, more controlled nature of the city may well have influenced them.

Conversely, many of these "advantages" were also contributing factors to the chasm that seemed to be developing between the African Americans in Aurora and the rest of the community. Like many of the immigrant groups, African Americans arrived as strange new people to be worked into the system in some way. Over time, Black families moved into formerly all-White neighborhoods, attended school with White children and worked alongside White men and women. But unlike the Germans, Swedes and Irish, true integration rarely took place. However slowly change may have occurred, European immigrants could become "Americanized" and join the dominant culture. African Americans could not change their race. As a result, though their economic standing improved, their social and political influence remained stagnant, or perhaps even dwindled at the beginning of the century.

The attributes that Palmer considered beneficial are precisely what Woodson identified as one of the great weaknesses of African Americans migrating North around the turn of the century:

> *Scattered through the North too in such small numbers, they have been unable to unite for social betterment and mutual improvement and naturally too weak to force the community to respect their wishes as could be done by a large group with some political or economic power.*[148]

From the collections of the Aurora Historical Society

An open street car, decorated for Labor Day, 1903. In the front of the car, just behind the policeman standing on the side step, is the only African American in the picture. That he stands out alone, even though his pose and attire are identical to the other middle class passengers, echoes Carter Woodson's words about black power being scattered and divided.

African Americans in Aurora seem to have been aware all along of their lack of power. Their very early efforts to distinguish themselves as capable of handling their own affairs were attempts to counter that situation. But as the community progressed and became more self-sufficient, what remained outside of their control was full acceptance into the life of the town. They watched as wave after wave of European immigrants moved in and gradually integrated into society. Meanwhile, in spite of their quick progress from slavery to vigorous citizenship, in 1920 the political structure and the inner circles of society remained closed to African Americans in Aurora.

The conflict between strongly stated and deeply cherished Jeffersonian beliefs on the one hand, and the day to day reality of racial bias and fear on the other, manifested itself in a cacophony of mixed signals. The White majority espoused the right of Black men to vote, but denied them full access to the political system. They professed the belief that Black labor was equal to White labor, then pigeonholed most African Americans into low paying, menial jobs. They advocated education for all, regardless of color, to make solid citizens for democracy, but taught the White youth to devalue the abilities of Black men and women.

The reactions of individuals in Aurora's Black community to wavering Republican ideology mirrored the strategies employed by African Americans over time and across the country to counter entrenched racism. Jim Meadows and Ben Mason seemed to play along with the stereotype of the "happy darkie." Whether they did so as a defense mechanism or as a means to get the better of pranksters by turning their own schemes back on them is uncertain. Isaiah Carter and

Calvin Boger sought equality and respect through economic means. Like many Black men of their era, their careers reflect the philosophy of Booker T. Washington. Hard work and quiet perseverance earned them public recognition and success in their businesses. However, recognition does not equal respect, and it does not necessarily imply equality. Calvin's son Henry, on the other hand, followed a path more in line with W.E.B. DuBois' counsel to the "Talented Tenth." Henry attended college and became a teacher. His letters from France show a growing political consciousness. Spurred by the sense that White men were devious and "crooked," Henry expressed a growing desire to agitate for the equality and justice that his father had tried to achieve through patience and restraint.

    And so we find that the route to glory doubled back. In 1867, Andy Lee wrote of entering political life under the aegis of "Radicalism." "With Radicalism to hold the light, I must look into society and make discoveries for its improvement."[149] Some fifty years later, Henry Boger and a generation of African American youth were questioning the status quo, and investigating the option of Radicalism, with the NAACP acting as their light. What they discovered was that there was considerable room for improvement in American society in 1920 and many hoped to begin a new reform.

Afterward

The photograph that graces the cover of this book is a compelling image. Carrie Jackson, a woman whose clothing and physical features suggest a life of work and worries, is caught in a moment of quiet reflection. She stares out the window, her eyes focused into the distance. One can imagine her pondering her past, with its troubles and triumphs. Or is she trying to imagine the future?

History is an endless process of looking backward to mark our journey. Looking back, though it can be difficult, often gives a sense of pride and accomplishment. But people can not move forward by looking only backward. The definition and purpose of history is to use the past to gain perspective on the present and create a vision for the future. While history does not have an end point, however, books must. The story of African Americans in Aurora is barely begun when this book concludes. Others will now have to pick up the story from here or add to our understanding of the story we thought we knew.

The Aurora Historical Society is trying to be a leader in this effort, as reflected in its mission statement:

> *The Aurora Historical Society, a public steward and educational resource, serves its community by collecting and preserving the documents and artifacts that reflect the richness and diversity of Aurora's history; by facilitating discovery and understanding of our shared history; and by taking a responsible role in the continued preservation and development of the community.*

The artifacts, photographs and documents gathered and preserved by AHS are more than a community attic. Collectively, they are a priceless resource held in public trust; the cornerstone of exhibits in two museums, as well as publications like this. The same materials are used regularly by students, genealogists, journalists, businesses, history buffs and professional historians to learn about their families, their neighborhoods and their community. The public programming and private research created with this collection shape Aurora's community identity.

To construct an accurate understanding of our shared history, the collection itself must reflect the full depth of Aurora's people. Very few people become famous, even in their own day, but their work, their entertainment, their lives are part of the larger fabric of this city. AHS continues to identify and preserve objects and documents of individuals and of local businesses and institutions because, as the collection grows, our ability to effectively interpret the past improves. To meet that challenge requires the cooperation and participation of the public. By reading this book, you have demonstrated an interest in Aurora's history. By donating photographs, clothing, letters, tools or other objects, you can participate in the ongoing effort to shape the future by preserving the past.

APPENDIX

THE AFRICAN AMERICAN POPULATION OF AURORA, AS ENUMERATED IN THE U. S. CENSUS

1850 Census

Last	First	Age	Relation	Occupation	Born	Address	Ward	Own/Rent	Literacy
	Phoebe	Unk	[Listed with Joseph Bora]		Unk				
	Gill	1	[Listed with Joseph Bora]		IL				

1860 Census

Last	First	Age	Relation	Occupation	Born	Address	Ward	Own/Rent	Literacy
Gillman	George	38	(white)	Laborer	MO				Illiterate
Gillman	Mary	38	Wife of George (mulatto)	Washerwoman	TN				Illiterate
Gillman	George	14	Son of George	Student	IL				
Gillman	Francis	6	Son of George		IL				
Gillman	Fredrick	3	Son of George		IL				
Gillman	Louis	3	Son of George		IL				
Parker	William	48			VA				
Demery	D	49		Whitewasher	TN				Illiterate
Demery	Julia	40	Wife of D.	Washerwoman	IL				Illiterate
Demery	Sarah	16	Daughter of D.	Washerwoman	Unk				
Demery	Charles	7	Son of D.		Unk				
Demery	Forman	5	Son of D.		Unk				
Demery	Emma	2	Daughter of D.		Unk				

1870 Census

Last	First	Age	Relation	Occupation	Born	Address	Ward	Own/Rent	Literacy
Warden	Alex	52		Laborer	KY	Unk.	Unk.	Own	
Warden	Melinda	20	Wife of Alex	Housekeeper	IL		Unk.		
Warden	Alex	12	Son of Alex	Student	WI		Unk.		
Warden	George	3	Son of Alex		IL		Unk.		
Warden	Willie	1	Son of Alex		IL		Unk.		
Landen	George	27		Laborer	MS	Unk.	Unk.	Unk.	
Landen	Lizzie	22	Wife of George	Housekeeper	MS		Unk.		
Landen	Frank	2	Son of George		IL		Unk.		
Landen	George	1	Son of George		IL		Unk.		
Sellen	Henry	20		Labor on Farm	TN	South city limits	Unk.	Unk.	
Palmer	G.W.	30		Laborer	TN	West May	1		Illiterate
Palmer	Mary	29	Wife of G.W.	Housekeeper	TN		1		Illiterate
Palmer	Laura	9	Daughter of G.W.	Student	TN		1		
Palmer	Henry	8	Son of G.W.	Student	IL		1		
Palmer	Kate	6	Daughter of G.W.		IL		1		
Palmer	George	3	Son of G.W.		IL		1		
Palmer	Oscar	1	Son of G.W.		IL		1		
DeCourcey	E.	14	Listed with F. Gridley		IL	12 Pine	1		Can't write
Bell	Samuel	40		Hostler	TN	9 Wilder	1	Own	
Bell	Maria	26	Wife of Samuel	Housekeeper	KY		1		
Bell	Alonzo	9	Son of Samuel	Student	MO		1		
Bell	Schuyler	1	Son of Samuel		IL		1		
Hunter	K.T.	24		Confectioner	GA	43 S. River	3		Can't write
Hunter	Hattie	19	Wife of K.T.	Housekeeper	IL		3		
Hodges	Sarah	24	Boarder	Domestic	IL		3		
Hodges	Josephine	6	Daughter of Sarah		IL		3		
Hodges	Mary	6 mo	Daughter of Sarah		IL		3		
Stanton	K.	20	Boarder		IL		3		
Stanton	[illegible]	2	Son of K.		IL		3		
Pride	George	30		Laborer	VA	South Lake	3	Unk.	Illiterate
Pride	Lizzie	25	Wife of George	Housekeeper	AL		3		Can't write
Pride	Robert	7	Son of George		IL		3		

141

1870 Census

Last	First	Age	Relation	Occupation	Born	Address	Ward	Own/Rent	Literacy
Pride	Sarah	4	Daughter of George		IL		3		
Pride	Delia	2	Daughter of George		IL		3		
Pride	Grant	10 mo	Son of George		IL		3		
Lamar	Mose	40		Laborer	AL	109 S. River	3	Unk.	
Washington	S.	24	With Ed Doty	Domestic	VA	18 River	3	Unk.	
Washington	J.	6	Daughter of S.		TX		3		
Blair	S.	26		Barber	PA	Unk.	3	Unk.	
Allen	William	59		Laborer	NC	South Lake	3		
Allen	T.Z.	53	Wife of Wm.	Housekeeper	AL		3		
Allen	Anne	22	Daughter of Wm.		AL		3		
Allen	Elsie	15	Daughter of Wm.		TX		3		Illiterate
Brown	George	23		Whitewasher	MS	South Lake	3		
Brown	M.	25	Wife of Geo.	Housekeeper	AL		3		
Brown	Hattie	1	Daughter of Geo.		IL		3		
Brown	Martha	4	Daughter of Geo		IL		3		
Hatton	George	40		Whitewasher	VA	South Lake	3	Unk.	Can't write
Hatton	Mary	30	Wife of Geo.	Housekeeper	KY		3		Illiterate
Hatton	Willie	4 mo	Son of Geo		IL		3		
Lane	Hannah	22	Boarder		AL		3		Can't write
LaMire	Mose	27		Laborer	AL	Unk.	3	Unk.	Illiterate
LaMire	Roxey	23	Wife of Mose	Housekeeper	AL		3		Illiterate
LaMire	Eddie	3			IL		3		
Luckett	Abe	27		Laborer	AL	South Lake	3	Unk.	Can't write
Luckett	P.	21	Wife of Abe		AL		3		Can't write
Luckett	Freddie	2	Son of Abe		IL		3		
Luckett	Jennie	9 mo	Daughter of Abe		IL		3		
Brown	F.	10							
Anthony	Frank	40		Laborer	MS	South Lake	3	Unk.	Illiterate
Anthony	Fannie	41	Wife of Frank		AL		3		Illiterate
Anthony	M.F.	14	Daughter of Frank		AL		3		Illiterate
Anthony	M.J.	13	Daughter of Frank		AL		3		Illiterate
Green	Hy	39		Laborer	VA	Unk.	4	Unk.	Illiterate

1870 Census

Last	First	Age	Relation	Occupation	Born	Address	Ward	Own/Rent	Literacy
Green	Anna	20	Wife of Hy	Housekeeper	KS		4		Illiterate
Porter	A.	18			KY		4		
Parks	Em	5	Ward/charge		IL		4		
Parks	Hellen	1	Ward/charge		IL		4		
Schell	S.	50		Laborer	KY	Unk.	4	Unk.	Illiterate
Schell	Mary	40	Wife of S.	Housekeeper	NC		4		Illiterate
Schell	Eliza	14	Daughter of S.		IL		4		
Schell	Robert	6	Son of S.		IL		4		
Schell	Charlie	4	Son of S.		IL		4		
Schell	Laura	10 mo	Daughter of S.		IL		4		
Thomas	S.M.	46		Laborer	D.C.	Claim & Beach	7	Unk.	
Thomas	Caroline	40	Wife of S.M.	Housekeeper	MD		7		
Thomas	S.M.	15	Son of S.M.		MA		7		
Thomas	Caroline	13	Daughter of S.M.	Student	Canada		7		
Moon	J.W.	24		Laborer	KS	Unk.	7	Unk.	
Moon	Sarah	25	Wife of J.W.	Domestic	KS		7		
Cole	Alex	11	Listed with Dr. Hamlin	servant	KS		7		
Meredith	Josesph	40		laborer	TN	19 Lincoln	8		
Meredith	Julie	42	Wife of Joseph	Housekeeper	MO	Unk.	8	Unk.	
Meredith	Garrison	12	Son of Joseph		MO		8		
Meredith	John	1 mo	Son of Joseph		IL		8		
Moore	James	26		Cook	WV	20 Main	9	Unk.	
Moore	Sarah	25	Wife of James	Housekeeper	OH		9		
Holland	Lizzie	20	Boarder		AL		9		
Holland	James	1 mo	Son of Lizzie		IL		9		
Mason	Henry	50		laborer	VA	South Water	9	Unk.	Illiterate
Mason	Jane	51	Wife of Henry	housekeeper	IL		9		
Mason	Henrietta	11	Daughter of Henry	Student	IL		9		
Mason	Emma	9	Daughter of Henry	Student	IL		9		
Mason	Willie	7	Son of Henry	Student	IL		9		
Mason	Horace	5	Son of Henry		IL		9		
Mason	Ben	2	White charge		IL		9		

1870 Census

Last	First	Age	Relation	Occupation	Born	Address	Ward	Own/Rent	Literacy
Mason	George	7 mo	White charge		IL		9		
Reddich	Thomas	25			KY	South Water	9	Unk.	
Reddich	Mary	24	Wife of Thomas		SC		9		Can't write
Lamar	Pete	40	Boarder	Laborer	TN		9		
Davis	Em	13	Listed with Ole Long	Domestic	VA	56 S. Broadway	9		
Davis	William	34		Laborer	KY	Unk.	9	Unk.	Illiterate
Davis	Sarah	30	Wife of Wm.	Housekeeper	AL		9		Illiterate
Davis	William	12	Son of Wm.		AL		9		
Davis	Ann	7	Daughter of Wm.		AL		9		
Davis	Harrison	4	Son of Wm.		IL		9		
Davis	John	1 mo	Son of Wm.		IL		9		
Davis	Mary	6	Daughter of Wm.		IL		9		
Martin	Thomas	30		Laborer	KY	South Lake	9	Unk.	
Martin	Ella	28	Wife of Thomas	Housekeeper	KY		9		
Martin	James	1			IL		9		
Demory	D.	54		Laborer	TN	South Water	9	Unk.	
Demory	Julia	50	Wife of D.	Housekeeper	IL		9		
Demory	Charles	18	Son of D.		IL		9		
Demory	Augustus	15	Son of D.		IL		9		
Demory	Louisa	12	Daughter of D.		IL		9		
Demory	Oscar	10	Son of D.		IL		9		
Demory	Isabella	8	Daughter of D.		IL		9		
Williams	J.P.	38		Barber Shop	Haiti	Fox east of bridge	9	Own	
Williams	Mary	39	Wife of J.P.	Housekeeper	IN		9		
Williams	Laura	2	Daughter of J.P.		IL		9		
Williams	Clara	9 mo	Daughter of J.P.		IL		9		
Leonard	Gerty	11	White charge		IL		9		
Meadows	James	37	Boarder		GA		9		
Carter	H.W.	28		Porter	KY	25 Water	9	Unk.	Illiterate
Carter	Lucy	21	Wife of H.W.	Housekeeper	KY		9		Illiterate
Carter	Emma	4	Daughter of H.W.		IL		9		
Carter	Willie	2	Son of H.W.		IL		9		

144

1870 Census

Last	First	Age	Relation	Occupation	Born	Address	Ward	Own/Rent	Literacy
Mahala	T.	20	Boarder		AL		9		
Thomas	S.	50		Laborer	D.C.	Unk.	9	Unk.	
Thomas	Caroline	40	Wife of S.	Housekeeper	D.C.		9		
Thomas	Sam	16	Son of S.		MA		9		
Thomas	Carrie	13	Daughter of S.		Canada		9		
Triggs	M.	53		Housekeeper	VA	Unk.	9	Unk.	
Triggs	Eugene	14	Son of M.		MS		9		
Hodges	James	30		Laborer	AL	161 S. LaSalle	9		
Hodges	Sarah	22	Wife of James	Housekeeper	IL		9		
Hodges	Josephine	7	Daughter of James	Student	IL		9		
Hodges	Mary	4 mo	Daughter of James		IL		9		
Stanton	Kate	19	Boarder		IL		9		
Stanton	Frank	3	Son of Kate		IL		9		
Webb	Mose	45		Barber	KY	18 Fox	9	Own	
Webb	Linda	26	Wife of Mose	Housekeeper	AL		9		
Ricks	Robert	20	Boarder	Barber	MO		9		
Green	H.	40		Laborer	D.C.	Unk.	9	Unk.	Illiterate
Green	Ann	20	Wife of H.	Housekeeper	TN		9		Illiterate
Parks	Alice	25	Boarder		AL	South LaSalle	9		
Parks	Emma	4	Daughter of Alice		IL		9		
Parks	Hellen	2	Daughter of Alice		IL		9		
Porter	Ann	18	Boarder		KY		9		
Porter	Louis	1 mo	Son of Ann		IL		9		Illiterate
Hayward	Eliza	15	Listed with J. Williams	Domestic	TN	69 S. LaSalle	9		
DeCourcey	Milton	38		Barber	OH	Allen Ave.	11	Own	
DeCourcey	Lydia	21	Wife of Milton	Housekeeper	IN		11		
DeCourcey	Ida	13	Daughter of Milton	Student	OH		11		
Rogers	William	20	Boarder	Barber	SC		11		
Recks	Robert	20	Boarder	Barber	TN		11		
Coleman	James	40		Laborer	VA	Unk.	11	Unk.	
Coleman	Mary	30	Wife of James	Housekeeper	VA		11		
Coleman	Ed	6	Son of James		IL		11		

145

1870 Census

Last	First	Age	Relation	Occupation	Born	Address	Ward	Own/Rent	Literacy
Coleman	Jane	3	Daughter of James		IL		11		
Edwards	I	30	Boarder	Laborer	VA		11		
Edwards	Ellen	29	Wife of I.	Housekeeper	VA		11		
Simmons	Sally	80	Boarder		VA		11		
Jones	Red	30		Laborer	TN	Unk.	11	Unk.	
Redd	Malachi	30		Laborer	KY	Grant Ave.	11	Unk.	
Redd	Georgie	29	Wife of Malachi	Housekeeper	VA		11		
Redd	Kate	5	Daughter of Malach		OH		11		
Redd	Lucy	3	Daughter of Malach		OH		11		
Coleman	Edmund			Stone Cutter		S. Anderson		Unk.	

1880 Census

Last Name	First Name	Age	Relation	Occupation	Born	Address	Ward	Literacy
Hughes	Jane	50	Listed with J. McGuire	Servant	TN	9 N. Lincoln	7(?)	Illiterate
DeCoursey	Edward	23		Hostler	OH	123 1st Ave.	10(?)	
DeCoursey	Lola	19	Wife of Edward	Housekeeper	IL			
DeCoursey	Carry	3	Daughter of Edward		IL			
DeCoursey	Maud	1	Daughter of Edward		IL			
Harding	Alexander	58		Laborer	KY	Unk.	Unk.	
Harding	Malinda	28	Wife of Alex	Housekeeper	IL			
Harding	George	12	Son of Alex	Student	IL			
Harding	William	10	Son of Alex	Student	IL			
Harding	Lilley	8	Daughter of Alex	Student	IL			
Harding	Mary	6	Daughter of Alex	Student	IL			
Harding	Centennial	4	Son of Alex		IL			
Harding	Julie	2	Daughter of Alex		IL			
Harding	Anna M.M.	2 mo	Daughter of Alex		IL			
Ridley	Joseph	56		Laborer	VA	Unk.	Unk.	
Ridley	[Illegible]	28	Wife of Joseph	Housekeeper	AL			
Ridley	Fred	13	Son of Joseph		IL			
Ridley	Jennie	11	Daughter of Joseph		IL			
Ridley	Ronnie	9	Son of Joseph	Student	IL			
Ridley	Henry	7	Son of Joseph		IL			
Ridley	Oliver	3	Son of Joseph		IL			
Ridley	Eva	5 mo	Daughter of Joseph		IL			
Hantz		32	Boarder	Laborer	GA			
Cooper	Gus	37		Laborer	VA	Unk.	Unk.	
Cooper	Anna	32	Wife of Gus	Housekeeper	AL			
Cooper	Clara	9	Daughter of Gus	Spinal disease	IL			
Cooper	Julia	7	Daughter of Gus	Student	IL			
Cooper	Stella	4	Daughter of Gus		IL			
Cooper	Peter M.	5 mo	Son of Gus		IL			
Hodges	John	35		Laborer	AL	Unk.	Unk.	
Hodges	Mary	35	Wife of John	Housekeeper	AL			
Hodges	Annie	12	Daughter of John		IL			

1880 Census

Last Name	First Name	Age	Relation	Occupation	Born	Address	Ward	Literacy
Hodges	John	10	Son of John	Student	IL			
Hodges	Eddie	8	Son of John	Student	IL			
Hodges	James	6	Son of John	Student	IL			
Hodges	George	4	Son of John		IL			
Watson	John	30	Boarder	Laborer	TN	Unk.	Unk.	Can't read
Catlett	William	25		Laborer	TN	Unk.	Unk.	Illiterate
Catlett	Liza	22	Wife of William	Housekeeper	TN			
Catlett	George	8	Son of William	Student	TN			
Catlett	Hatty	6	Daughter of William	Student	TN			
Jones	Martha	54	Widow	Housekeeper	KY	Unk.	Unk.	Can't read
Perry	George	20		Barber	IN	Unk.	Unk.	
Perry	Isabell	18	Wife of George	Housekeeper	IL			
Perry	Eda	7 mo	Daughter of George		IL			
Demmery	Oscar	21	Listed with R. Northam	Servant	IL	12 Fox	Island	Illiterate
Lamar	Peter	45		Laborer	MS	Unk.	Island	Illiterate
Bell	Samuel	45		Laborer	TN	Wilder & Vine	1	
Bell	Ann M.	38	Wife of Samuel	Housekeeper	KY		1	
Bell	Schuyler	11	Son of Samuel	Student	IL		1	
Bell	John	7	Son of Samuel	Student	IL		1	
Bell	Lottie	5	Daughter of Samuel		IL		1	
Allen	William	34		Laborer	AL	North May	1	Illiterate
Allen	Kate	30	Wife of Wm.	Housekeeper	AL		1	Illiterate
Allen	Harrison	12	Son of Wm.	Student	IL		1	
Allen	William	9	Son of Wm.	Student	IL		1	
Allen	Fred	6	Son of Wm.	Student	IL		1	
Allen	Joe	3	Son of Wm.		IL		1	
Allen	Virgil	4 mo	Son of Wm.		IL		1	
Allen	William	70	Father of Wm.	Laborer	NC		1	Illiterate
Allen	Theresa	50	Mother of Wm.	Housekeeper	NC		1	Can't write
Shell	Solomon	57		Laborer	KY	River & Gale	3	Illiterate
Shell	Mary	52	Wife of Solomon	Housekeeper	TN		3	Illiterate
Shell	Robert	17	Son of Solomon	Laborer	IL		3	

1880 Census

Last Name	First Name	Age	Relation	Occupation	Born	Address	Ward	Literacy
Shell	Laura	12	Daughter of Solomon	Student	IL		3	
Shell	Daniel	8	Son of Solomon		IL		3	
Taylor	E.	35		Laborer	KY	19 S. Lake	3	Illiterate
Taylor	Johanna	34	Wife of E.	Washerwoman	AL		3	Illiterate
Taylor	Dora	18	Daughter of E.	Washerwoman	IL		3	
Taylor	Nellie	12	Daughter of E.	Student	IL		3	
Taylor	Lena	10	Daughter of E.	Student	IL		3	
Taylor	Fannie	7	Son of E.	Student	IL		3	
Taylor	Frank	5	Daughter of E.		IL		3	
Taylor	Mamie	2			IL		3	
Sadler	Hannah	30		Housekeeper	AL	21 S. Lake	3	Illiterate
Sadler	William	10	Son of Hannah	Student	IL		3	
Sadler	Albert	8	Son of Hannah	Student	IL		3	
Sadler	John	5	Son of Hannah	Student	IL		3	
Sadler	Nora	2	Daughter of Hannah		IL		3	
Lamar	Mose	36		Laborer	Unk.	21 S. Lake	3	
Lamar	Celia	26	Wife of Mose	Housekeeper	Unk.		3	
Lamar	Nellie	4	Daughter of Mose		Unk.		3	
Lamar	Elle	2	Daughter of Mose		Unk.		3	
[Illegible]	John	7	Brother		Unk.		3	
[Illegible]	[Illegible]	32	Brother		Unk.		3	
Martin	Thomas	40		Laborer	AL	23 S. Lake	3	Illiterate
Martin	Alice	40	Wife of Thomas	Housekeeper	AL		3	Illiterate
Martin	Emma	13	Daughter of Thomas	Student	IL		3	
Martin	[Illegible]	12	Daughter of Thomas	Student	IL		3	
Mason	Henry	58		Laborer	VA	17 S. Lake	3	Illiterate
Mason	Anne	40	Wife of Henry	Housekeeper	IL		3	
Mason	Henrietta	21	Daughter of Henry	Washerwoman	IL		3	
Mason	Emma	20	Daughter of Henry		IL		3	
Mason	Willie	17	Son of Henry	Laborer	IL		3	
Mason	Florence	15	Daughter of Henry	Servant	IL		3	
Mason	Ben	13	Son of Henry	Laborer	IL		3	

149

1880 Census

Last Name	First Name	Age	Relation	Occupation	Born	Address	Ward	Literacy
Mason	Eva	9	Daughter of Henry	Student	IL		3	
Mason	May	3	Daughter of Henry		IL		3	
Mason	Florence	15	REAPEAT	Servant, Fitch	IL		3	
Palmer	Laura	17	Listed with Geo. Bauer?	Servant	IL	Rural near 2nd	5	
Wortham	Wesley	50	Listed with P. Phelps	Servant	NC	Liberty	6	
Merriweather	Alfred	27		Laborer	KY	37 N. Broadway	7	
Merriweather	Salina	28	Wife of Alfred	Housekeeper	TN		7	
Merriweather	Anna	6	Daughter of Alfred		TN		7	
Merriweather	Thomas	3	Son of Alfred		TN		7	
Merriweather	Cornealius	10 mo	Son of Alfred		IL		7	
Catlett	Catherine	53	Widow	Washerwoman	TN	100 Spring	7	Illiterate
Catlett	Elisa	21	Daughter of Catherine	Washerwoman	TN		7	Illiterate
Catlett	Harry	19	Son of Catherine	Cook	TN		7	Illiterate
Catlett	George	13	Son of Catherine	Student	TN		7	Illiterate
Moon	Porge	46	Boarder	Laborer	VA		7	Illiterate
Moon	Bertha	32	Wife of Porge	Washwoman	TN		7	Illiterate
Moon	Katton	12	Daughter of Porge	Student	TN		7	
Moon	William	10	Son of Porge	Student	TN		7	
Moon	Gustav	9	Son of Porge	Student	TN		7	
Moon	Page	6	Son of Porge	Student	TN		7	
Moon	James	5 mo	Son of Porge		TN		7	
Hunter	King G.	28		Laborer	KY	121 Main	8	Can't read
Hunter	Hattie	28	Wife of King	Housekeeper	IL		8	
Hunter	Minnie	9	Daughter of King	Student	IL		8	
Hunter	Lorla	4	Daughter of King		IL		8	
Hunter	Geneva	2	Daughter of King		IL		8	
Adams	John	39		Roofer	AK	171 S. River	8	Illiterate
Adams	Drusella	29	Wife of John	Housekeeper	AL		8	Illiterate
Adams	Henry	14	Son of John	Student	IA		8	
Adams	Charles	9	Son of John	Student	IL		8	
Adams	Roy	5	Son of John		IL		8	
Brown	John	47	Boarder	Laborer	KY		8	Illiterate

1880 Census

Last Name	First Name	Age	Relation	Occupation	Born	Address	Ward	Literacy
Artis	Clinton	41		Upholsterer	IN	101 Spring	8	Illiterate
Artis	Cornelia	39	Wife of Clinton	Housekeeper	D.C.		8	Illiterate
Artis	George	22	Son of Clinton	Laborer	IL		8	Can't read
Artis	Annie	19	Daughter of Clinton	Student	IL		8	
Artis	Willis	18	Son of Clinton	Laborer	IL		8	
Artis	Edward	15	Son of Clinton	Student	IL		8	
Artis	Pearl	4	Daughter of Clinton		IL		8	
Hardin	George	14	Listed with Fred Pond	Laborer & Student	IL	Root & Short	8	
Demery	Charles	27		Laborer	IL	20 S. Anderson	9	
Demery	Jennie	26	Wife of Charles	Housekeeper	VA		9	
Demery	Gus	25	Brother of Chas.	Laborer	IL		9	
Carter	Susan	18	Wife of Ben	Housekeeper	TN	Broadway/Benton	9	Can't write
Carter	Benjiman	29		Laborer	Unk		9	Illiterate
Meadows	James	48		Laborer	"south"	8 S. LaSalle	9	Illiterate
Meadows	Liddia	34	Wife of James	Housekeeper	"south"		9	Illiterate
Meadows	Robert	19	Stepson James		IL		9	
Meadows	Sarah	15	Stepdaughter James	Student	IL		9	
Meadows	Delia	12	Stepdaughter James	Student	IL		9	
Meadows	Grant	10	Stepson James	Student	IL		9	
Meadows	James	6	Son of James	Student	IL		9	
Meadows	Sherman	4	Son of James		IL		9	
Meadows	Wallace	2	Son of James		IL		9	
Ward	Henry	44		Cook, Tremont	MD	30 S. Water	9	
Austin	Ambrose	37		Runner, Fitch	VA	29 S. Water	9	Illiterate
Meredith	Joseph	35		Laborer	VA	20 Main	9	Illiterate
Meredith	Julia	40	Wife of Joseph	Housekeeper	MO		9	Illiterate
Meredith	Garrison	20	Son of Joseph	Laborer	MO		9	
Meredith	George	10	Son of Joseph	Student	IL		9	
Meredith	Julia	7	Daughter of Joseph	Student	IL		9	
Meredith	Joseph	4	Son of Joseph		IL		9	
Webb	Mose	53		Barber	KY	49 S. Broadway	9	
Webb	Mary	35	Wife of Mose	Housekeeper	Prussia		9	

151

1880 Census

Last Name	First Name	Age	Relation	Occupation	Born	Address	Ward	Literacy
Webb	Peter	14	Son of Mose		WI		9	
Webb	Maggie	12	Daughter of Mose		WI		9	
Webb	Annie	5	Daughter of Mose		IL		9	
Sanders	William	43	Boarder	Barber	MD		9	
Tinsley	James	39	Boarder	Barber	KY		9	
Jackson	William	41		Laborer	KY	Benton & Water	9	
Jackson	Caroline	40	Wife of William	Housekeeper	TN		9	
Wethers	Joseph	20	Boarder	Laborer	VA		9	
Hollis	George	39	Boarder	Laborer	TN		9	
Grinton	Eva	16	Listed with Rev Tucker	Servant	IL	16 S. LaSalle	9	
Gavney	Sylvia	63	Listed with Rev Tucker	Servant	VA	16 S. LaSalle	9	
Lucas	Ann	39	Widow	Housekeeper	VA	17 S. Lincoln	9	Can't write
Lucas	Thomas	20	Son of Ann	Laborer	D.C.		9	Can't write
Ford	Martha	33	Boarder		AL		9	Can't write
Mason	William	18	Listed with N. Goldsmith	Servant	IL	Fourth & Benton	9	Can't write
Smith	Mattie	30	Widow	Housekeeper	KY	25 S. Water	9	Illiterate
Lindsay	Fanny	65	Widow/boarder		KY		9	Illiterate
Austin	Mary	36	Wife of Ambrose	Housekeeper	MO	29 S. Water	9	Illiterate
Austin	Dora	5 mo	Daughter of Ambrose		IL		9	
Austin	Allie	2	Daughter of Ambrose		IL		9	
Ward	Henry	46		Cook	MD	30 S. Water	9	
Ward	Kate	27	Wife of Henry	Housekeeper	IN		9	
Ward	Gertie	10	Daughter of Henry	Student	OH		9	
Lucas	Thomas	20		Horstler	VA	83 S. Lincoln	9	
Bibbs	William			Laborer		32 Main	9	
Demery	Louise	21		Laundress, Fitch	IL		9	
Palmer	Washington	40		Works in tile factory	TN	2nd & East Ave.	10	Illiterate
Palmer	Mary	37	Wife of Wash.	Housekeeper	TN		10	Illiterate
Palmer	Larry	18	Son of Wash	[Illegible]	TN		10	
Palmer	Henry	17	Son of Wash	Works in tile factory	IL		10	
Palmer	Katie	15	Daughter of Wash	Student	IL		10	
Palmer	Gary	12	Son of Wash	Student	IL		10	

1880 Census

Last Name	First Name	Age	Relation	Occupation	Born	Address	Ward	Literacy
Palmer	Oscar	10	Son of Wash	Student	IL		10	
Palmer	Jessie	8	Daughter of Wash	Student	IL		10	
Palmer	Gracie	3	Daughter of Wash		IL		10	
Palmer	Angel	6 mo	Son of Wash		IL		10	
Brooks	Perry	43		White washer	KY	Fifth Ave.	10	Illiterate
Brooks	Luzi	33	Wife of Harry	Housekeeper	KY		10	Illiterate
Brooks	Marie	14	Daughter of Harry	Student	IL		10	
Brooks	William	12	Son of Harry	Student	IL		10	
Brooks	Gertrude	9	Daughter of Harry	Student	IL		10	
Brooks	Della	6	Daughter of Harry		IL		10	
Brooks	Cornelia	1	Daughter of Harry		IL		10	
Edwards	William	38		Teamster	VA	Fifth Ave.	10	Illiterate
Edwards	Mary	34	Wife of Wm.	Housekeeper	KY		10	Illiterate
Edwards	Frank	16	Son of Wm.	Wks w/ father	IL		10	
Edwards	Anna	14	Daughter of Wm.	Student	IL		10	
Edwards	Jennie	10	Daughter of Wm.	Student	IL		10	
Edwards	Fred	4	Son of Wm.		IL		10	
Edwards	Cora	2	Daughter of Wm.		IL		10	
Williams	Albert	40		Cook	MO	Unk.	11	
Williams	Laura	29	Wife of Albert	Housekeeper	TN		11	
Williams	Hattie	13	Daughter of Albert	Student	MI		11	
Williams	George	11	Son of Albert	Student	MI		11	
Williams	James	9	Son of Albert	Student	IL		11	
Williams	May	4	Daughter of Albert		IL		11	
Williams	David	1	Son of Albert		IL		11	
Williams	Adale	3 mo	Daughter of Albert		IL		11	
Boger	Calvin	35		Stone Mason	GA	Grove near Beach	11	
Boger	Amy	31	Wife of Cal	Housekeeper	IL		11	
Boger	Harry	8	Son of Cal	Student	IL		11	
Boger	Blanch	4	Daughter of Cal		IL		11	
Boger	Maud	1	Daughter of Cal		IL		11	
Hall	John	34	Brother-in-law	Barber	IL		11	

153

1880 Census

Last Name	First Name	Age	Relation	Occupation	Born	Address	Ward	Literacy
Williams	Albert	46		Cook, Fitch	MO	North Ave.	11	
DeCoursey	Milton	45		Barber	IL	7 Allen	11	
DeCoursey	Nettie	34	Wife of Milton	Housekeeper	IN		11	
DeCoursey	Eva	16	Daughter of Milton	Dress maker	IL		11	
Edwards	Peter	50		Laborer	NC	Talma near Gifford	11	
Edwards	Hannah	40	Wife of Peter	Washwoman	AL		11	
Bibbs	Louisa	20	Daughter of William Bibbs	Housekeeper	AL		11	
Bibbs	Gracie	1	Granddaughter of Wm. Bibbs		IL		11	

1900 Census

Last Name	First Name	Age	Relation	Occupation	Born	Address	Ward	Own/Rent	Literacy
Jones	James	51		Farmer	TN	Farm	Twp	Rent farm	
Jones	Nora	22	Wife of James		MI		Twp		
Johnson	James	24		Chemical Works	MS		Twp	Rent	
Johnson	Ethel	20	Wife of James		TN		Twp		
LeMar	Mamie	16	Listed with Katherine Gould	Domestic servant	IL		Twp		
Catlett	Catherine	70	Widow		TN		Twp	Mortgage	Illiterate
Catlett	George	29	Son of Catherine	Day laborer	TN		Twp		
Mayweather	Alfred	46		Couple-binder	TN		Twp	Rent	Illiterate
Mayweather	Lena	47	Wife of Alfred	Wash woman	TN		Twp		
Mayweather	Cornelius	20	Son of Alfred	Day laborer	IL		Twp		
Mayweather	Tabbie	17	Daughter of Alfred	Servant	IL		Twp		
Catlett	John	49		Plasterer	TN		Twp	Own	
Catlett	Margret	34	Wife of John		MO		Twp		
LeMar	James	73		Farm laborer	AL		Twp	Own	Can't write
LeMar	Ella	46	Wife of James		VA		Twp		Can't write
LeMar	Emanuel	28	Son of James	Porter	VA		Twp		
LeMar	Mary	16	Daughter of James	Servant	IL		Twp		
LeMar	Norma	8	Daughter of James	Student	IL		Twp		
Robinson	Elizabeth	23	Daughter of James/wid.	Servant	IL		Twp		
Robinson	William	8	Grandson of James	Student	IL		Twp		
Duke	Matthew	34	(white)	Day laborer	TN		Twp	Rent	
Duke	Anna	26	Wife of Matthew		TN		Twp		
Duke	Leroy	8	Son of Matthew	Student	IL		Twp		
Duke	Thomas	4	Son of Matthew		IL		Twp		
Duke	Myrtle	2	Daughter of Matthew		IL		Twp		
Duke	Earnest	3 mo	Son of Matthew		IL		Twp		
Carter	Bennett	49		Plasterer	TN		Twp	Own	
Carter	Susan	37	Wife of Bennett		TN		Twp		
Carter	Shuster	18	Son of Bennett	Day laborer	IL		Twp		
Carter	Pearl	17	Daughter of Bennett	House keeper	IL		Twp		
Carter	Isaiah	15	Son of Bennett	Bell boy	IL		Twp		
Carter	Ollie	13	Son of Ben	Student	IL		Twp		
Carter	Cornelius	10	Son of Ben	Student	IL		Twp		

1900 Census

Last Name	First Name	Age	Relation	Occupation	Born	Address	Ward	Own/Rent	Literacy
Carter	Blanche	9	Daughter of Ben	Student	IL		Twp		
Carter	Lute	7	Daughter of Ben	Student	IL		Twp		
Carter	Bennett	5	Son of Ben		IL		Twp		
Carter	Clyde	1	Son of Ben		IL		Twp		
Carter	Charles	50		Baptist Minister	OH	Farm	Twp	Mortgage on farm	
Carter	Rosa	46	Wife of Charles		IL		Twp		
Douglas	Edward	35		Day laborer	VA		Twp	Rent	
Douglas	Catherine	32	Wife of Edward		TN		Twp		
Douglas	Edward	9	Son of Edward	Student	IL		Twp		
Douglas	Ralph	3	Son of Edward		IL		Twp		
Belle	Lutheran	24		Day laborer	MO		Twp	Rent	
Belle	Malinda	17	Wife of Lutheran		IL		Twp		
Moore	Elizabeth	50	Widow		TN		Twp	Mortgage	Illiterate
Moore	Page	26	Son of Elizabeth	Day laborer	TN		Twp		
Moore	James	20	Son of Elizabeth	Day laborer	TN		Twp		
Moore	Fred	17	Son of Elizabeth	Day laborer	IL		Twp		
Moore	Bessie	15	Daughter of Elizabeth	Student	IL		Twp		
Moore	Clarence	12	Son of Elizabeth		IL		Twp		
Harding	Alexander	85		White washer	KY		Twp	Own	Illiterate
Harding	Malinda	50	Wife of Alexander		MO		Twp		
Harding	Gertrude	12	Daughter of Alexander	Student	IL		Twp		
Jackson	Caroline	60	Widow	Washerwoman	TN		Twp	Mortgage	Illiterate
Johnson	Charles	46	Widower	Laborer	TN		Twp	Rent	Illiterate
Johnson	Alice	14	Daughter of Charles	Student	IA		Twp		
Johnson	Aurelia	13	Daughter of Charles	Student	KS		Twp		
Johnson	Daniel	9	Son of Charles	Student	IL		Twp		
Harding	William	30		Coachman	IL		Twp	Rent	
Harding	Georganna	30	Wife of William		PA		Twp		
Harding	Lillian	12	Daughter of William	Student	IL		Twp		
Harding	Golda	9	Daughter of William	Student	IL		Twp		
Warren	Edward	46		Laborer	MS		Twp	Own	
Warren	Cynthia	38	Wife of Edward		MO		Twp		
Warren	Clara	17	Daughter of Edward	Student	IL		Twp		Illiterate

1900 Census

Last Name	First Name	Age	Relation	Occupation	Born	Address	Ward	Own/Rent	Literacy
Warren	Edward	12	Son of Edward	Student	IL		Twp		
Henderson	Alexander	15	Boarder (white)	Student	Scot.		Twp		Arr. 1888
Ran	Frank	Unk	Boarder (white)	Farm laborer			Twp		
Jackson	Charles	38		Shoe maker	AL		1	Rent	
Jackson	Harriet	37	Wife of Charles		TN		1		
Hilliard	Ann M.	60	Widow		KY		1	Rent	Can't write
Hilliard	William H.	28	Son of Ann	Janitor	IL		1		
Hilliard	Nellie	29	Daughter-in-law		IL		1		
Hilliard	Lottie	7	Granddaughter		IL		1		
Hilliard	Alice	6	Granddaughter		IL		1		
Carter	Martha	56	Widow		KY		1	Rent	Illiterate
Carter	Jim	33	Son of Martha	Janitor	KY		1		
Carter	John	31	Son of Martha	Coachman	KY		1		
Hurbut	Mary	16	Granddaughter		KY		1		
Durrett	Charity	26	Daughter of Martha		KY		1		
Bell	Samuel	70		Day laborer	TN		1	Own	Illiterate
Bell	Maria	49	Wife of Sam		KY		1		
Bell	John	24	Son of Sam	Day laborer	IL		1		
Bell	Samuel	21	Son of Sam	Ice man	IL		1		
Bell	Elizabeth	18	Daughter-in-law	Teamster	IN		1	Own	
Allen	Harrison	31			KY		1		
Allen	Amanda	31	Wife of Harrison		IL		1		
Allen	Grant	10	Son of Harrison	Student	IL		1		
Allen	Roy	7	Son of Harrison	Student	IL		1		
Allen	Willie	5	Son of Harrison		IL		1		
Allen	Clarence	2	Son of Harrison		IL		1		
Goodchild	Paris	54		Day laborer	MO		1	Rent	
Holland	Lizzie	54	Widow	Servant/housekeeper	AL		1		Illiterate
LaMar	Emanuel	27	Boards w/ E. Puffer	Porter	IL		2	Rent	
LaMar	Joseph	23		Hotel runner	IL		2		
LaMar	Hattie	20	Wife of Joseph		IL		2		
LaMar	Mable	6 mo	Daughter of Joseph		IL		2		
Warne	Spencer	28	Boarder	Coachman	AL		2		

1900 Census

Last Name	First Name	Age	Relation	Occupation	Born	Address	Ward	Own/Rent	Literacy
Robinson	Lizzie	24	Sister of Joseph	Char woman	IL		2		
Demery	Edward	44		Day laborer	IL		2	Rent	Illiterate
Demery	Jane	38	Wife of Edward		VA		2		
Webb	Emma	21	Listed with Upshaw Hord	Servant/domestic	KY		2		
Jackson	Daisy	21	Listed with Ben Brenner	Servant/housekeeper	IN		2		
Webb	Mary	41	Listed with Edmond Raftery	Domestic servant	VA		2		
Robinson	John	53		Day laborer	AL		2	Rent	Illiterate
Robinson	Pamela	49	Wife of John	Laundress	KY		2	Rent	Illiterate
Dyer	Charles	29		Laborer	MI		2	Rent	
Dyer	Alberta	29	Wife of Charles		MI		2		
Kipper	Edward	42		Day laborer	MO		2	Rent	Illiterate
Kipper	Ella	30	Wife of Edward		MO		2		
Kipper	Bessie	1	Daughter of Edward		IL		2		
Hunter	James	40		Stool Works employee	VA		2	Rent	
Hunter	Jessie	25	Wife of James		IL		2		
Hunter	Mabel	5	Daughter of James		IL		2		
Allen	Virgil	21	Listed with Walter Frazier	Servant	W. Indies		2		
White	James	63		Pensioner	ME		2	Rent	
White	Mary	43	Wife of James	Washwoman	MD		2		
Johnson	Thomas	36		Stove polisher	IL		2	Rent	
Johnson	Effie	29	Wife of Thomas		AL		2		
Warren	Spencer	28	Listed with Lincoln Frazier	Servant	IL		2		
Jackson	Florence	25	Listed with Lysander Hord	Servant/domestic	IL		2		
Burnett	Antony	54	Listed with Lysander Hord	Servant	SC		2		
Cooper	Thomas	59		Laborer	VA		2	Own	
Cooper	Lucy	39	Wife of Thomas, 9 years		MO		2		
Cooper	John	20	Son of Thomas	Laborer	IL		2		
Cooper	Lois	14	Daughter of Thomas	Student	IL		2		
Cooper	Paul	7	Son of Thomas & Lucy	Student	IL		2		
Edwards	Peter	66		Day laborer	SC		3	Rent	Illiterate
Edwards	Rosa	Unk	Wife of Peter		VA		3		Can't write
Catlett	William	44		Day laborer	TN		3	Mortgage	Illiterate
Catlett	Lizzie	Unk	Wife of William		VA		3		Illiterate

1900 Census

Last Name	First Name	Age	Relation	Occupation	Born	Address	Ward	Own/Rent	Literacy
Catlett	George	27	Son of William	Day laborer	TN		3		
James	Alonzo	39		Janitor	MO		3	Own	
James	Adel	35	Wife of Alonzo		IA		3		
Edwards	William	66		Farmer	VA		3	Own farm	
Edwards	Mary	Unk	Wife of William		KY		3		Illiterate
Edwards	Cora	21	Daughter of William	Housework	IL		3		
Edwards	George	16	Son of William	Farm laborer	IL		3		
Brooks	Perry	62		Day laborer	KY		3	Mortgage	
Brooks	Lucy	54	Wife of Perry		KY		3		Illiterate
Brooks	Cornelia	21	Daughter of Perry	Housework	IL		3		Illiterate
Johnson	Willus	10	Stepson	Student	IL		3		
White	Frank	36		Brick Baker	IL		3	Rent	
White	Jennie	33	Wife of Frank		IL		3		
White	Hazel	14	Daughter of Frank	Student	IL		3		
White	Owen	12	Son of Frank	Student	IL		3		
White	Edith	10	Daughter of Frank	Student	IL		3		
White	Ruth	1	Daughter of Frank		IL		3		
Roberts	Rosa	37	Listed with George Howard	Servant	IL		3		
Wilson	Ida	30		Washing & ironing	TN		3	Rent	Illiterate
Wilson	Howard	30	Boarder	Stone mason	OH		3		
Meredith	Joseph	24		Day laborer	IL		4	Rent	
Meredith	Rosa	22	Wife of Joseph		IA		4		
Williams	Caroline	58	Mother, widowed	Day laborer	MO		4		
Johnson	Della	20	Listed with John Love	Servant/domestic	IL		4		
Morton	John	35		Caterer/restaurant	VA		4	Rent	
Morton	Fanny	26	Wife of John		IA		4		
Morton	Theodore	11	Son of John	Student	IL		4		
Norwood	Rachel	43	Married	Domestic servant	MO		4	Rent	Illiterate
Norwood	Georgie	8	Daughter of Rachel	Student	IA		4		
McGruder	Elmira	26	Niece (married)	Domestic servant	MO		4		
Matthew	Robert	30	Boarder	House painter	MO		4		
Martin	Thomas	60		Day laborer	TN		4	Rent	Illiterate
Martin	Alice	50	Wife of Thomas		AL		4		Illiterate

1900 Census

Last Name	First Name	Age	Relation	Occupation	Born	Address	Ward	Own/Rent	Literacy
Lucas	Eugene	11	Grandson	Student	IL		4		
Lee	David	28	Son-in-law of Thomas	Day laborer	MO		4		
Lee	Helen	30	Daughter of Thomas		IL		4		
Hatten	George	70	Widower	Day laborer	MD		4	Rent	Can't write
LaMar	Peter	63	Partner of George	House janitor	AL		4		Illiterate
LaMar	Katie	47	Wife of Peter		MA		4		
Dare	William	30	Boarder	House janitor	IL		4		
Henderson	Buster	35		Day laborer	VA		4	Rent	
Henderson	May	35	Wife of Buster		TN		4		Illiterate
Henderson	Andrew	20	Son of May	Day laborer	IL		4		
Henderson	Harry	16	Son of May	Day laborer	IL		4		
Henderson	James	6	Son of May		TN		4		
Lucas	Alfred	42		Patrol Driver	KY		4	Mortgage	
Lucas	Emma	34	Wife of Alfred		IL		4		
Lucas	Perl	10	Daughter of Alfred	Student	IL		4		
Hunter	King G.	54		Day laborer			4	Own	
Hunter	Hattie	42	Wife of King		IL		4		
Hunter	Verna	13	Daughter of King	Student	IL		4		
Boyde	Nathaniel	28	Boarder	Day laborer	IL		4		
[Illegible]	Gelma	3	Niece of King		IL		4		
Franklin	Benjamin	53		Day laborer	TN		4	Rent	
Franklin	Altha	46	Wife of Ben		AL		4		
Franklin	Henry	23	Son of Ben	Servant	IL		4		
Franklin	Robert	19	Son of Ben	Day laborer	AL		4		
Franklin	Lizzie	14	Daughter of Ben	Student	IL		4		
Franklin	Walter	10	Son of Ben	Student	IL		4		
Franklin	Eddie	7	Son of Ben	Student	IL		4		
Parmer	Washington	61		Teamster	TN		4	Rent	
Parmer	Mary A.	58	Wife of Washington		TN		4		
Parmer	Edward	19	Son of Washington	Brick maker	IL		4		
Parmer	Mattie	14	Granddaughter	Student	IL		4		
Parmer	Mertie	12	Granddaughter	Student	IL		4		
Spriggs	William	42		Laundryman	VA		5	Rent	

1900 Census

Last Name	First Name	Age	Relation	Occupation	Born	Address	Ward	Own/Rent	Literacy
Spriggs	Nora	22	Wife of William		IL		5		
Spriggs	William	3	Son of William		IL		5		
Spriggs	Mildred	2	Daughter of William		IL		5		
Powell	Hanna	49	Mother-in-law		AL		5		Illiterate
Gigger	Emma	53	Widow	Hairdresser	IN		5	Rent	Illiterate
Gigger	Lizzie	29	Daughter of Emma/wid.	Housekeeper	IL		5		
Haris	Edward	32	Boarder/widower	Servant	TN		5		
McKan	Arthur	26	Boarder	Day laborer	IL		5		
White	Alice	48	Boarder	Carpet weaver	VA		5		
Manning	George	23	Boarder	Housekeeper	MI		5		
Bell	Kellie	27		Coal miner	KS		5	Rent	
Redford	Andrew	34	Boarder	Washwoman	MS		5		Illiterate
Meredith	Julia	53	Widow		MO		5	Rent	Illiterate
Meredith	Julia	20	Daughter of Julia	Porter	IL		5		
Meadows	James	26			IL		5	Rent	
Meadows	May	23	Wife of James		IL		5		
Meadows	Mildred	2	Daughter of James		IL		5		
Meadows	Beatrice	5 mo	Daughter of James	Porter	IL		5		
Meadows	Wallace	21	Brother of James	Proprietor, candy shop	IL		5		
Webb	Moses	74		Domestic	KY		5	Mortgage	Illiterate
McCann	Annie	35	Live-in servant	Barber	TN		5		
Watson	Frank	64			PA		5	Rent	
Watson	Louisa	50	Wife of Frank	Drives grocery wagon	AL		5		
Moore	William	30			TN		5	Rent	
Moore	Lillie	28	Wife of William		IL		5		
Moore	Adaline	6	Daughter of William		IL		5		
Moore	Vernie	2	Son of William	Tar roofer	IL		5		
Adams	H.W.	34		Student	IL		5	Rent	
Adams	Florence	34	Wife of H.W.	Student	IL		5		
Adams	Clifford	11	Son of H.W.	Weaver	IL		5		
Sargeant	Olivia	13	Adopted daughter		IN		5		
Long	Samuel	34			AL		5	Rent	
Long	Sarah	32	Wife of Samuel		IL		5		

161

1900 Census

Last Name	First Name	Age	Relation	Occupation	Born	Address	Ward	Own/Rent	Literacy
Long	Charley	15	Son of Samuel	Wool cutter	IL		5		
Meadows	Eva	18	Sister-in-law		IL		5		
Meadows	Pearl	12	Niece	Student	IL		5	Rent	
Malone	John W.	69		Minister	NC		5		
Malone	Margaret	52	Wife of John		MO		5		
Adams	Liza	48	Widow		AL		5	Rent	
Adams	Charles	29	Son of Liza	Gravel roofer	IL		5		
Adams	Roy	25	Son of Liza	Gravel roofer	IL		5		
Renfro	Edna	25	Listed with William Wilson	Domestic/housekeeper	IL		5		
Reed	Joe	28	Wife of Joe	Hostler	KY		6	Rent	
Reed	Cornelia	23	Wife of Joe		IL		6		
Reed	Paul	1	Son of Joe		IL		6		
Wright	Jane	59	Widow	Washer woman	IL		6	Rent	
Butler	Emma	39	Daughter of Jane		IL		6		
Bogar	Calvin	50		Contractor/mason	GA		6	Own	
Bogar	Amy	51	Wife of Calvin		IL		6		
Bogar	Harry	28	Son of Calvin	Mason	IL		6		
Bogar	Maude	20	Daughter of Calvin	Student	IL		6		
Bogar	Calvin	17	Son of Calvin	Mason/plasterer	IL		6		
Bogar	Thomas	14	Son of Calvin	Student	IL		6		
Bogar	Henry	12	Son of Calvin	Student	IL		6		
Bogar	Delphia	10	Daughter of Calvin	Student	IL		6		
Bogar	Amy	7	Daughter of Calvin	Student	IL		6		
Artist	Clinton	46		Day laborer	AL		6	Rent?	Illiterate
Artist	Corinia	49	Wife of Clinton		AL		6		Illiterate
Artist	George	21	Son of Clinton	Day laborer	IL		6		
Wallace	Samuel	53		Barber	Mexico		6	Rent	
Wallace	Laurie	42	Wife of Samuel		IL		6		
Wallace	Francis	16	Daughter of Samuel		IL		6		
Richards	Charles	51		Laborer	VA		7	Rent	
Richards	Laura	37	Wife of Charles		VA		7		Illiterate
Richards	George	15	Son of Charles	Farm laborer	VA		7		
Richards	Ollie	8	Son of Charles	Student	IL		7		

162

1900 Census

Last Name	First Name	Age	Relation	Occupation	Born	Address	Ward	Own/Rent	Literacy
Richards	Carry	6	Daughter of Charles	Student	IL		7		
Richards	Robert	3	Son of Charles		IL		7		
Washington	George	49		Laborer, street	VA		7	Rent	Can't write
Washington	Hattie	39	Wife of George	Washing & ironing	TN		7	Rent	
Smith	Henry	33		Teamster	IL		7		
Smith	Maggie	28	Wife of Henry		IL		7		
Smith	Lizzie	10	Daughter of Henry	Student	IL		7		
Smith	Ivy	7	Daughter of Henry		IL		7		
Smith	Ward	5	Son of Henry		IL		7		
Smith	Wilbur	4	Son of Henry		IL		7		
Smith	Amelia	2	Daughter of Henry		IL		7		
Vaughn	Thomas	34		Teamster	VA		7	Mortgage	
Vaughn	Carrie	34	Wife of Thomas		VA		7		
Vaughn	Guy	8	Adopted son of Thomas	Student	IA		7		
Goodrich	Simon	34	Boarder	Barber	VA		7		
Johnson	Louis	43		Teamster	NC		7	Rent	
Johnson	Martha	50	Wife of Louis		GA		7		

1910 Census

Last Name	First Name	Age	Relation	Occupation	Born	Address	Ward	Own/Rent	Literacy
Kelly	Fred	30	Listed with Sarah Beckwith	Domestic servant	IA	110 Palace	1		
Bell	Samuel	38		Engineer/mfg. co.	IL	75 Vine	1	Mortgage	
Bell	Elizabeth	27	Wife of Samuel		IN		1		
Bell	Gwendolyn	6	Daughter of Samuel		IL		1		
Bell	Winifred	3	Daughter of Samuel		IL		1		
Grimes	Oscar	26	Listed with A.J. Hopkins	Domestic servant	WI	47 N. Lake	1		
Grimes	Nellie	25	Wife of Oscar	Domestic servant	IA		1		
Hunter	James	49		Laborer/mfg. Co.	WV	9 Galena	1	Rent	
Hunter	Jessie	26	Wife of James		IL		1		
Hunter	Mable	14	Daughter of James		IL		1		
Hunter	Joseph	5	Son of James		IL		1		
Johnson	James	40		Fireman/Hotel Arlington	Unk	9-11 N. River	1		
Patterson	Rose	23	Listed with Charles Earl	Servant	KY	288 Grand	1	Rent	
Tayler	William	35		Coachman	KS	275 N. Lake	1		
Tayler	Eva	35	Wife of William		IL		1		
Martinez	Garfield	28	Brother-in-law	Polisher, flat irons	IL		1		
Barbee	Ola	20	Listed with John Newhall	Servant	KY	333 Galena	1		
Durette	James	39		School janitor	KY	485 Charles	1	Own	
Durette	Hattie	29	Wife of James		KY		1		
Allen	Harrison	41		Sand pit	IL	122 May	1	Own	
Allen	Manda	42	Wife of Harrison		IL		1		
Allen	Grant	21	Son of Harrison	Works with father	IL		1		
Allen	Roy	17	Son of Harrison	Laborer	IL		1		
Allen	Willie	15	Son of Harrison	Laborer	IL		1		
Allen	Clarence	12	Son of Harrison	Student	IL		1		
Allen	Flossie	9	Daughter of Harrison	Student	IL		1		
Allen	Alberta	5	Daughter of Harrison		IL		1		
Allen	Virgil	30	Married	Cleaner/housework	IL	120 May	1	Own	
Allen	Rosie	28	Sister of Virgil		IL		1		
Allen	Helen	8	Daughter of Virgil		IL		1		
Allen	Katherina	6	Daughter of Virgil		IL		1		
Patterson	Alex	35		Laborer/odd jobs	KY	270 View	1	Mortgage	
Patterson	Cora	31	Wife of Alex		KY		1		

1910 Census

Last Name	First Name	Age	Relation	Occupation	Born	Address	Ward	Own/Rent	Literacy
Patterson	Frances	15	Daughter of Alex		KY		1		
Patterson	Cecilia	3	Daughter of Alex		IL		1		
Smith	Earl	20	Nephew of Alex	Laborer/odd jobs	KY		1		
Bridgford	Leona	28	Married		MO	402 Highland	1	Own	
Bridgford	Burnell	14	Son of Leona		MO		1		
Bridgford	Fay	12	Son of Leona		MO		1		
Bridgford	Agnes	10	Daughter of Leona		MO		1		
Bridgford	Fanny	6	Daughter of Leona		IL		1		
Bridgford	Paul	4	Son of Leona		IL		1		
Hardin	John	32		Driver @ cooperage	KY	332 Gillette	1	Rent	
Hardin	Bettie	22	Wife of John		KY		1		
Harding	Leadre	2	Son of John		KY		1		
Abrams	Wilbur	44		Janitor/domestic	SC	535 W. Park	1	Own	
Abrams	Lulu	35	Wife of Wilbur		GA		1		
Abrams	Archie	18	Son of Wilbur	Trucking manufacturing	AL		1		
Abrams	William	16	Son of Wilbur		IL		1		
Abrams	Armon	11	Son of Wilbur		IN		1		
Allen	Stella	6	Niece of Wilbur		AL		1		
Jones	James	32		Teamster @ lumber co.	IL	380 Gillette	1	Mortgage	
Jones	Stella	29	Wife of James		IL		1		
Jones	Irene	6	Daughter of James		IL		1		
Jones	Lillian	2	Daughter of James		IL		1		
Johnson	Fanny	51	Mother-in-law/widow	Nurse/private family	VA		1		Illiterate
Palmer	Edna	26	Sister-in-law				1		
Jones	Amelia	54	Mother		IL		1		Illiterate
Palmer	Bernice	2	Niece		WV		1		
Hunter	James	49		Laborer, mfg. co.	IL		1	Rent	
Hunter	Jessie	26	Wife of James		IL		1		
Hunter	Mable	14	Daughter of James		IL		1		
Hunter	Joseph	5	Son of James		IL		1		
Long	Samuel	Unk		Barber shop	AL	52 Galena	2	Own	
Long	Sara	Unk	Wife of Samuel	Dressmaker	IL		2		
Carlyle	Clara	18	Listed with E.S. Hanna	Servant/housework	KY	309 Downer	2		

1910 Census

Last Name	First Name	Age	Relation	Occupation	Born	Address	Ward	Own/Rent	Literacy
Wright	Jane	70	Widow	Scrub woman, corset co.	IL	9 Holbrook	2	Rent	
Buttler	Emma	49	Daughter of Jane	Porter @ saloon	IL		2		
Demery	Charles	57	Brother of Jane, wid.		IL		2		
Hunter	Thomas	36		Laborer @ McCarty	KY	48 Galena	2	Rent	
Hunter	Flora	36	Wife of Thomas		IL		2		
Hunter	Ilva	13	Daughter of Thomas		KY		2		
Hunter	Alena	12	Daughter of Thomas		KY		2		
Hunter	Thomas	10	Son of Thomas		KY		2		
Lindsay	Jerdan	37	Boarder	McCarty Improve Co.	OH		2		
Stewart	Will	26	Boarder		IL		2		
Cooper	Thomas	69		Gardener	VA	580 Garfield	2	Own	
Cooper	Francis	49	Wife of Thomas	Asphalt/paver	MO		2		
Cooper	John	29	Son of Thomas	Polisher, stove works	IL		2		
Cooper	Paul	18	Son of Thomas		IL		2		
Scott	George	33		Laborer/odd jobs	KY	438 Ogden	2	Rent	
Scott	Nancy	32	Wife of George		KY		2		
Scott	Ward	11	Son of George		IL		2		
Scott	Pauline	9	Daughter of George		IL		2		
Scott	Elmer	7	Son of George		IL		2		
Scott	Valor	2	Son of George		IL		2		
Adams	Howard	33		Laborer/odd jobs	IA	420 Ogden	2	Rent	
Adams	Ada	24	Wife of Howard		Can		2		
Perkins	Elizabeth	35	Widow	Washerwoman/odd jobs	KY	378 Ogden	2	Rent	
Warren	Spencer	39		Laborer/private family	LA	182 Smith	2	Rent	
Warren	Lizzie	35	Wife of Spencer	Laundress/odd jobs	IL		2		
Warren	William	17	Son of Spencer	Laborer/odd jobs	IL		2		
Edwards	Anne	23	Listed with Adam Bleitz	Servant (divorced)	KY	811 S. Lake	2		
Johnson	Tom	45		Factory labor	MD	249 Middle	2	Rent	
Johnson	Effie	35	Wife of Tom		IL		2		
Johnson	Margorie	7	Daughter of Tom		IL		2		
Noble	Orrin	27		Teamster, barrel mfr.	IL	300 S. Lake	2	Rent	
Noble	Alice	22	Wife of Orrin		IL		2		
Franklin	Henrietta	33	Listed with E.S. Frazier	Domestic servant	AL	5th Ave.	2		

1910 Census

Last Name	First Name	Age	Relation	Occupation	Born	Address	Ward	Own/Rent	Literacy
Robinson	John	50	Widower	Laborer/odd jobs	U.S.	319 S. River	2	Rent	
Harmon	Jessie	35	Boarder, divorced	Laborer/odd jobs	MA		2		
Fort	Columbia	36	Boarder with Dan Foster	Cement worker	U.S.	River Road	2		
Carter	Mable	16	Listed with Lars Bodinson	Domestic servant	TN	272 Seminary	3		
Roberts	Rose	46	Listed with George Howard	Domestic servant	IL	268 Weston	3		
McCann	Arthur	37		Church janitor	IL	319 Rosewood	3	Mortgage	
McCann	Lizzie	38	Wife of Arthur		IL		3		
Scott	Mable	20	Step-daughter		IL		3		
Wallace	Samuel	62		Barber shop	PA	421 S. Broadway	3	Mortgage	
Wallace	Louisa	51	Wife of Samuel		IL		3		
Wallace	Frances	27	Daughter of Samuel	Dressmaker shop	IL		3		
Morton	John	44		Caterer	VA	414 Rosewood	3	Mortgage	
Morton	Frances	36	Wife of John		IA		3		
Morton	John	21	Son of John	Steward	IL		3		
Morton	Martha	5	Daughter of John		IL		3		
Catlett	William	52		Labor for contractor/mason	TN	340 Talma	3	Own	
Catlett	Eliza	52	Wife of William		VA		3		
Mayweather	Alberta	13	Granddaughter		IL		3		
Jackson	Minnie	52	Boarder	Teacher industrial school	KY		3		
Dyer	Charles	37		Dry goods store clerk	MI	473 Jackson	3	Own	
Dyer	Alberta	36	Wife of Charles		MI		3		
Dyer	Erieta	7	Daughter of Charles		IL		3		
Dyer	Walter	6	Son of Charles		IL		3		
Teackle	Frances	95	Grandmother		VA		3		
Russ	Adelia	58	Mother-in-law, widow		MD		3		
Strong	Samuel	31		Waiter	TN	421 Watson	3	Own	
Strong	Annie	30	Wife of Samuel		IL		3		
Strong	Bessie	12	Daughter of Samuel		AS		3		
Edwards	William	75		Laborer/City of Aurora	VA	707 5th Ave.	3	Own	
Brown	Mattie	48	Sister-in-law		KY		3		
Edwards	Fred	34	Son of William	Laborer/private farm	IL		3		
Brooks	Lucy	66			KY	911 5th Ave.	3	Own	
Brooks	Mary	43	Daughter	Domestic servant	IL		3		

1910 Census

Last Name	First Name	Age	Relation	Occupation	Born	Address	Ward	Own/Rent	Literacy
Brooks	Coarie	40	Son	Coachman, private	IL		3		
James	Alonso	48		Carpet layer/dry goods	MO	482 Watson	3	Own	
James	Adel	44	Wife of Alonso		IA		3		
James	Dorothy	11	Daughter of Alonso		IL		3		
Jackson	C.	72	Listed with Carrie Potter	Servant, boarding home	TN	98 Lincoln	4		
Wilson	S.M.	50	Widow	[illegible]	IL	72 North Ave.	4	Own	
Wilson	Bert	18	Son	[porter in Dir]	IL		4		
Mayweather	C.	30		Moulder/foundry	IL	70 North Ave.	4	Own	
Mayweather	Emma	31	Wife		KY		4		
Mayweather	Alveda	9	Daughter		IL		4		
Nelson	Gust.	39		Porter/laborer	TN	64 North Ave.	4	No info given	
Nelson	Mary	37	Wife		TN		4		
Anderson	Mary	26	Niece	Theatre	MS		4		
Blackman	Mary	57	Widow	Washer woman	TN	25 Clark	4	Rent	Illiterate
Blackman	James	18	Son	Laborer	IL		4		
Hill	Joe	52		Laborer/paving	TX	Clark	4	Rent	
Bell	John H.	20	Boarder	Laborer	MS		4		
Martin	Thomas	75		Roofer	TN	29 Clark	4	Rent	
Martin	Alice	60	Wife of Thomas		AL		4		
Lucas	Lujane	21	Grandson	Night watch/factory	IL		4		
Smith	Henry	45			IL	119 Stone	4	Rent	
Smith	Margarite	40	Wife of Henry	Domestic servant	IL		4		
Smith	Elizabeth	20	Daughter of Henry	Laborer/factory	IL		4		
Smith	Ward	16	Son of Henry		IL		4		
Smith	Amelia	12	Daughter of Henry		IL		4		
Smith	Camilla	6	Daughter of Henry		IL		4		
Smith	Marilu	2	Daughter of Henry		IL		4		
Buckner	W.	50		Moulder/stove works	MS	127 Stone	4	Rent	
Buckner	Josephine	40	Wife	Scrub floors, offices	AL		4		
Buckner	Mary	16	Daughter		IL		4		
Buckner	Mary	74	Mother		AL		4		Illiterate
Taylor	Susetti	34	Listed with Alexander Forsyth	Domestic servant	KY	70 Root St.	4		
Lamar	Emanuel	34		Porter in saloon	IL	446 North Ave.	4	Mortgage	

1910 Census

Last Name	First Name	Age	Relation	Occupation	Born	Address	Ward	Own/Rent	Literacy
Lamar	Sophia	30	Wife of Emanuel		LA		4		
Lamar	Wiliam	1	Son of Emanuel		IL		4		
Washington	George	69		Laborer/odd jobs	VA	650 North Ave.	4	Rent	
Washington	Hattie	49	Wife of George		TN		4		
Adams	Charles	42		Tar roofer	IL		4	Mortgage	
Adams	Florence	40	Wife of Charles		IL		4		
Young	William	45	Boarder	Fireman for City	TN		4		
Hunter	Hattie	52	Widow		TN	625 Benton	4	Mortgage	
Muse	Josephine	Unk	Boarder	Laundress	Unk		4		
Muse	Marie	Unk	Boarder	Teacher, public school	Unk		4		
Muse	Ernest	27	Boarder	Barber	Unk		4		
Muse	Allis	20	Wife of Ernest		Unk		4		
Muse	Mildrede	3	Daughter of Ernest		Unk		4		
Simmons	Frank	34		Teamster	IL	604 2nd Ave.	4	Rent	
Simmons	Mary	36	Wife of Frank		VA		4		
Simmons	Cora	15	Daughter of Frank		IL		4		
Simmons	Elma	12	Daughter of Frank		IL		4		
Simmons	Lanaria	9	Daughter of Frank		IL		4		
Simmons	Albertha	7	Daughter of Frank		IL		4		
Simmons	[Illegible]	5	Daughter of Frank		IL		4		
Simmons	Margaret	6 mo	Daughter of Frank		IL		4		
Spriggs	Elnora	32	Widow	Domestic/housework	IL	54 N. Lincoln	5	Rent	
Spriggs	Mildred	11	Daughter of Elnora		IL		5		
Spriggs	William	13	Son of Elnora		IL		5		
Spriggs	Norman	5	Son of Elnora		IL		5		
Powell	Hanna	56	Widow, mother of Elnora		AL		5		
Young	George	30	Boarder	Laborer/street	IL		5		
Harris	Lee	23	Boarder	Fireman @ factory	OH		5		
Giger	Emma	60		Keeps boarding house	IN	58 N. Lincoln	5	Rent	
Spriggs	Katy	39	Daughter of Emma		IL		5		
Spriggs	William	43	Son-in-law of Emma	Laborer/coal yard	OH		5		
Williams	John	76	Boarder		VA		5		
Lewis	Edward	35	Boarder	Porter @ saloon	IL		5		

1910 Census

Last Name	First Name	Age	Relation	Occupation	Born	Address	Ward	Own/Rent	Literacy
Lewis	Jean	27	Boarder	Porter @ saloon	IL		5		
Curry	Ray	18	Boarder	Porter @ club	OH		5		
Curry	Fred	21	Boarder	Laborer/street	OH		5		
Straun	Theo	19	Boarder	Porter/barber shop	IL		5		
Perdue	Edward	27	Boarder	Fireman, school house	IL		5		
Marshall	Lidiya	64	Widow		AL	53 LaSalle	5	Rent	Illiterate
Parker	William	50	Boarder	Laborer/odd jobs	WV		5		Illiterate
Moreland	James	24	Boarder	Laborer/paving co.	IA		5		
Johnson	Jennett	23		Housework @ home	KY	137 Main	5	Rent	
Aust	Pearl	30		Housework, private family	IN	137 Main	5	Rent	
Aust	Louisa	14	Daughter of Pearl		IN		5		
Aust	Harlin	13	Son of Pearl		IN		5		
McDonald	Mary	55	Mother of Pearl		IN		5		Illiterate
Simons	Edward	27		Porter @ saloon	IL	137 Main	5	Rent	
Simons	Anna	22	Wife of Edward		IL		5		
Simons	Violet	2	Daughter of Edward		IL		5		
Simons	Edward	7 mo	Son of Edward		IL		5		
Spencer	Joe	29		Cook @ café	MD	137 Main	5	Rent	
Spencer	Blanche	27	Wife of Joe		KY		5		
Wells	Beatriss	27	Widow	Keeps boarding house	MO	109 Spring	5	Rent	Illiterate
Wilford	Simon	Unk	Boarder	Hod carrier for mason	Unk		5		
Porter	Ben	Unk	Boarder	Hod carrier for mason	Unk		5		
Rollins	Jess	Unk	Boarder	Roofer, roofing co.	Unk		5		
Campbell	Joe	Unk	Boarder	Hod carrier for mason	Unk		5		
Caseson	Tomas	Unk	Boarder	Laborer/foundry	KY		5		
Plowden	Robert	Unk		Cook @ saloon	Unk	111 Spring	5	Rent	
Edwards	Fred	30	Listed with Timothy Holden	Hired man/gardener	IL	793 5th Ave.	5	Rent	
Webb	Moses	85	Widower	Candy store proprietor	KY	391 New York	5	Mortgage	Illiterate
McCann	Annie	57	Live in servant	Domestic	TN		5		
Gaines	George	62		Minister	MS	543 Main	5	Mortgage	
Palmer	George	60		Teamster, coal co.	TN	15 East Ave.	5	Rent	
Palmer	Mary	45	Wife of George		TN		5		
Douglas	Ed	45		Teamster, coal co.	IL	17 East Ave.	5	Rent	

1910 Census

Last Name	First Name	Age	Relation	Occupation	Born	Address	Ward	Own/Rent	Literacy
Douglas	Catherine	42	Wife of Ed		IL		5		
Douglas	Eddie	19	Son of Ed	Laborer on farm	IL		5		
Douglas	Ralph	13	Son of Ed		IL		5		
Russel	Will	39		Barber shop	IL	570 Benton	5	Own	
Russel	Daisy	32	Wife of Will		IL		5		
Russel	Charles	6 mo	Son of Will		IL		5		
Russel	Willie	3	Son of Will		IL		5		
Jackson	Esther	21	Sister-in-law	Domestic servant	IL		5		
Moore	William	40		Driver for grocer	TN	16 East Ave.	5	Mortgage	
Moore	Lilly	38	Wife of William		IL		5		
Moore	Adalade	15	Daughter of William	Student	IL		5		
Moore	Verne	13	Son of William	Student	IL		5		
Adams	Mary	32	Listed as married	Housework	KY	11 East Ave.	5	Own	
Seldon	John	38		Mason	AL	13 East Ave.	5	Rent	
Seldon	Effie	30	Wife of John		MS		5		
Seldon	Artarene	7	Daughter of John		IL		5		
Cantrell	Charles H.	43		Janitor/housework	TN	208 Root St.	6	Rent	
Cantrell	Liveana	34	Wife of Charles		TN		6		
Cantrell	Nettie	13	Daughter of Charles		TN		6		
Cantrell	Virginia	10	Daughter of Charles		TN		6		
Cantrell	Mary	22	Step-daughter	Housework	TN		6		
Boger	Calvin	64		Mason & contractor	GA	228 Claim	6	Own	
Boger	Amy	61	Wife of Calvin		IL		6		
Boger	Calvin	27	Son of Calvin	Bricklayer	IL		6		
Boger	Hazel	20	Daughter-in-law of Calvin		MO		6		
Boger	Thomas	23	Son of Calvin	Barber	IL		6		
Boger	Amy	19	Daughter of Calvin		IL		6		
Lewis	Allen	47	White	Cabinet maker	MO	266 College	6	Rent	
Lewis	Mary	46	Wife of Allen (mullato)	Cook/private family	MO		6		
Lewis	Roberta	12	Step-daughter		IL		6		
Lewis	Corine	15	Step-daughter	Domestic servant	IL		6		
Artis	Cornelius	72			D.C.	488 Spring	6	Own	
Webb	Hugh	26	Son-in-law	Porter/laborer	KY		6		

171

1910 Census

Last Name	First Name	Age	Relation	Occupation	Born	Address	Ward	Own/Rent	Literacy
Webb	Hazel	23	Daughter		IL		6		
Hunter	Edna	34	Daughter (married)				6		
Hall	Elisha	53		Janitor/Daily News	IL	231 Beach	6	Mortgage	
Hall	Isabel	41	Wife of Elisha		IL		6		
Hall	[Illegible]	15	Son of Elisha		IL		6		
Hall	Marguerite	11	Daughter of Elisha		IL		6		
Washington	Mary	66	Mother-in-law	Widow	AL		6		
Walkup	Peter	30		Porter/laborer	KY	571 Kane	6	Mortgage	
Walkup	Pearl	23	Wife of Peter		IL		6		
Vaughn	Thomas	46		Teamster/coal co.	IL	197 Superior	7	Own	
Vaughn	Kate	47	Wife of Thomas		VA		7		
Webb	Jeff	38		Hod carrier for contractor	IL	174 Superior	7	Rent	
Webb	Lillie	37	Wife of Jeff		IL		7		
Webb	Mamie	16	Daughter of Jeff	Bell boy @ hotel	IL		7		
Webb	Blanche	14	Daughter of Jeff		IL		7		
Webb	Rendy	12	Daughter of Jeff		IL		7		
Webb	Coy	7	Son of Jeff		IL		7		
Webb	Ella	4	Daughter of Jeff		IL		7		
Riggs	William	42		Teamster/coal co.	IA	174 Superior	7	Rent	
Riggs	Anna	41	Wife of William		Unk		7		
Davy	Fred	23	Boarder	Laborer/McCarty Co.	IA		7		
Jordan	William	34	Boarder	Plasterer/contractor	IL		7		
Hays	Robert	26		Laborer/house cleaner	IN	274 Beach	7	Rent	
Hays	Amanda	31	Wife of Robert		KY		7		
Hays	Sadie	15	Daughter of Robert	Student	KY		7		
Carlyle	Ferris	26	Boarder	Laborer/hod carrier	KY		7		
Porter	Ben	32	Boarder	Laborer/hod carrier	MS		7		
Duke	Matthew	44		Laborer/brick yard	TN	Indian Ave.	7	Rent	
Duke	Leroy	18	Son of Matthew	Laborer/brick yard	IL		7		
Duke	Thomas	14	Son of Matthew		IL		7		Illiterate
Duke	Myrtle	11	Daughter of Matthew		IL		7		
Duke	Ernest	10	Son of Matthew		IL		7		
Duke	Mildred	8	Daughter of Matthew		IL		7		

1910 Census

Last Name	First Name	Age	Relation	Occupation	Born	Address	Ward	Own/Rent	Literacy
Duke	Lila	6	Daughter of Matthew		IL		7		
Matthews	Alydia	19	Housekeeper	Domestic servant	IL		7		

1920 Census

Last	First	Age	Relation	Occupation	Born	Address	Ward	Own/Rent	Literacy
Edwards	John	44		Laborer	KY	Walnut	Twp.	Rent	
Edwards	Sarah	35	Wife of John	Laborer/laundress	KY		Twp.		
Edwards	William E.	17	Son of John		KY		Twp.		
Edwards	Mary	14	Daughter of John		KY		Twp.		
Powell	John	24	Employed by Elizabeth Wick	Chauffeur	FL		Twp.	Unknown	
Griffin	John	52		Section hand	MI	Fifth	Twp.	Own free	
Griffin	Ollie	34	Wife of John		KY		Twp.		
Griffin	Hortence	5	Daughter of John		IL		Twp.		
Jackson	Charles	55		Laborer/Railroad	VA	Montgomery Rd	Twp.	Own free	
Jackson	Hattie	46	Wife of Charles		VA		Twp.		Illiterate
Catlett	George	50		Laborer/Gas company	KY	Montgomery Rd	Twp.	Own free	
Catlett	Dora	40	Wife of George		IL		Twp.		
Catlett	Gilbert	5	Son of George		IL		Twp.		
Cantrell	Charles	54		Janitor at bank	TN	235 View	1	Mortgage	
Cantrell	Leenona	44	Wife of Charles		TN		1		
Barrigher	Annett	23	Daughter of Charles		TN		1		
Barrigher	Francis	25	Son-in-law	Operator/wire mills	NY		1		
Barrigher	Francis	1	Grandson of Charles		IL		1		
Bridgeford	Ester	45		Janitor/Telephone co.	MO	301 View	1	Own free	
Bridgeford	Bettie	42	Wife of Ester		MO		1		
Bridgeford	Elsie	22	Daughter of Ester		MO		1		
Kelly	Fred	44		Laborer/Foundry	IA	223 Hammond	1	Mortgage	
Kelly	Lucetta	44	Wife of Fred	Laundress at home	KY		1		
Kelly	William	5	Son of Fred		KY		1		
Durham	John	23	Nephew	Waiter at Elk's Club	KY		1		
Durham	Ozella	18	Niece		AL		1		
Miller	Lester	21	Listed with John P. Love	Laborer/Private home	IL	473 N. Lake	1		
Hix	Burt	33	Listed with Beverly Waters	Laborer/Private home	TX	523 N. Lake	1		
Hardin	John	41		Laborer/Iron company	KY	323 View	1	Own free	
Hardin	Bettie	32	Wife of John		KY		1		
Hardin	Leander	12	Son of John		KY		1		
Hardin	Gertrude	7	Daughter of John		IL		1		
Durrette	John	39		Janitor/Private home	KY	139 May St.	1	Own free	

1920 Census

Last	First	Age	Relation	Occupation	Born	Address	Ward	Own/Rent	Literacy
Durrette	Agnes	39	Wife of John		MO		1		
Bridgeford	John	26	Brother-in-law	Machinist/Steel co.	MO		1		
Bridgeford	Irene	23	Sister-in-law		MO		1		
Durrette	James	53		Janitor/Private home	KY	485 Charles	1	Mortgage	
Durrette	Hattie	42	Wife of James		KY		1		
Simms	John	29		Laborer/mfg. plant	KY	270 View	1	Rent	
Simms	Mary	20	Wife of John		IL		1		
Taylor	Robert	25	Brother-in-law	Laborer/Cooperage	IL		1		
Patterson	A. A.	40		Painter/Buildings	KY	274 View	1	Own free	
Patterson	Chlora	41	Wife of A. A.		KY		1		
Patterson	Carilie	12	Daughter of A. A.		IL		1		
Durham	John	62	Father-in-law		KY		1		
Patterson	Alex	35		Laborer/Odd jobs	KY	270 View	1	Mortgage	
Patterson	Cora	31	Wife of Alex		KY		1		
Patterson	Frances	15	Daughter of Alex		KY		1		
Patterson	Cecilia	3	Daughter of Alex		IL		1		
Smith	Earl	20	Nephew	Laborer/Odd jobs	KY		1		
Bridgeford	Lona	28	See Mitchell Bridgeford		MO	402 Highland	1	Own free	
Bridgeford	Burnell	14	Son of Lona		MO		1		
Bridgeford	Fay	12	Daughter of Lona		MO		1		
Bridgeford	Agnes	10	Daughter of Lona		MO		1		
Bridgeford	Fanny	6	Daughter of Lona		IL		1		
Bridgeford	Paul	4	Son of Lona		IL		1		
Hardin	John	32		Driver/Cooperage	KY	332 Gillette	1	Rent	
Hardin	Bettie	22	Wife of John		KY		1		
Hardin	Leander	2	Son of John		KY		1		
Abrams	Wilbur	44		Janitor/Private home	SC	535 W. Park	1	Own free	
Abrams	Lulu	35	Wife of Wilbur		GA		1		
Abrams	Archie	18	Son of Wilbur	Trucking/Mfg. co.	AL		1		
Abrams	William	16	Son of Wilbur		IL		1		
Abrams	Armon	11	Son of wilbur		IN		1		
Allen	Stella	6	Niece		AL		1		
Jones	James	32		Teamster/Lumber co.	IL	380 Gillette	1	Mortgage	

175

1920 Census

Last	First	Age	Relation	Occupation	Born	Address	Ward	Own/Rent	Literacy
Jones	Stella	29	Wife of James		IL		1		
Jones	Irene	6	Daughter of James		IL		1		
Jones	Lillian	2	Daughter of James		IL		1		
Johnson	Fanny	51	Mother-in-law	Nurse/Private family	VA		1		Illiterate
Palmer	Edna	26	Sister-in-law		IL		1		
Jones	Amelia	54	Mother		TN		1		Illiterate
Palmer	Bernice	2	Niece		IL		1		
Gien	James	30		Cook/Restaurant	TN	33 River St.	2	Rent	
Gien	Arvella	27	Wife of James	Dish washer	KY		2		
Branch	Will	30	Boarder	Barber	IL		2		
Jones	Rollin	42		Laborer	IL	49 Galena	2	Rent	
Jones	Lina	34	Wife of Rollin	Domestic servant	KY		2		
Jones	Tom	36		Laborer/Street car	KY	48 Galena	2	Rent	
Howard	Glen	19	Boarder	Helper/Barber shop	KY		2		
Malicoat	Mary	53	Boarder		PA		2		
Barnet	Sarah	43	Employed by W. S. Frazier	Domestic servant	KY	121 Indiana	2	Unknown	
Richmond	Scott	37	Employed by John Alexander	Domestic servant	WI	379 Hardin	2	Unknown	
Richmond	Pearl	30	Wife of Scott	Domestic servant	IL		2		
Zigler	Mary	56	Employed by P. H. Cooper	Domestic servant	MO	152 S. Broadway	2	Unknown	Illiterate
Zigler	Elizabeth	21	Listed with William Evans	Domestic servant	IL	529 Garfield	2	Unknown	
Wright	Jane	80	Widow		IL	9 Holbrook	2	Rent	
Wright	Elberta	57	Daughter of Jane	Labor/Cotton mill	IL		2		
White	Mary	60	Widow	Helper/Factory	KY	9 Holbrook	2	Rent	
Williams	Ethel	30	Listed with Emmitt Beckwith	Domestic servant	IA	304 Garfield	2	Unknown	
Grimes	Lulu	35	Listed with Thomas Stewart	Domestic servant	IA	264 Garfield	2	Live in	
Lewis	George	29		Teamster/Coal yard	IN	401 Ogden	2	Rent	
Lewis	Clara	25	Wife of George		IN		2		
Lewis	Marvin	6	Son of George		IN		2		
Lewis	Bertha	5	Daughter of George		IN		2		
Lewis	Elnora	4	Daughter of George		IN		2		
Lewis	Randall	8 mo.	Son of George		IL		2		
Robinson	Lewis	35		Laborer/Factory	KY	231 Middle	2	Unknown	
Robinson	Anna	20	Wife of Lewis		KY		2		

1920 Census

Last	First	Age	Relation	Occupation	Born	Address	Ward	Own/Rent	Literacy
Robinson	Harry	2	Son of Lewis		IL		2		
Johnson	Thomas	45		Laborer/Stove works	MD	249 Middle	2	Rent	
Johnson	Effie	40	Wife of Thomas		IL		2		
Johnson	Marjorie	16	Daughter of Thomas		IL		2		
Warren	Spencer	49		Janitor/Hardware mfr.	AL	182 Woodlawn	2	Rent	
Warren	Elizabeth	44	Wife of Spencer	Janitor/Hardware mfr.	IL		2		
Warren	William	28	Son of Spencer		IL		2		
Warren	Edna	23	Daughter-in-law		IL		2		
Warren	Iona	6	Daughter of Spencer		IL		2		
Warren	William	4	Grandson		IL		2		
Hunter	Thomas	45		Porter/Saloon	KY	451 Ogden	2	Rent	
Hunter	Flora	47	Wife of Thomas		IL		2		
Hunter	Thomas	19	Son of Thomas		KY		2		Illiterate
Hazelwood	Robert	42		Chauffeur/Coal truck	KY	455 Ogden	2	Rent	
Hazelwood	Georgia	27	Wife of Robert		KY		2		
Hazelwood	Linda	6	Daughter of Robert		KY		2		
Hazelwood	Edward	33		Chauffeur/Coal truck	KY	455 Ogden	2	Rent	
Hazelwood	Minnie	27	Wife of Edward		KY		2		
Hazelwood	Margaret	7	Daughter of Edward		KY		2		
Hazelwood	Edna	5	Daughter of Edward		KY		2		
Hazelwood	Adaline	4	Daughter of Edward		IL		2		
Hazelwood	Minnie	2	Daughter of Edward		IL		2		
Hazelwood	Dorothy	4 mo.	Daughter of Edward		IL		2		
Murdock	James	29		Laborer/Steel cabinet co.	KY	487 S. River St.	2	Rent	
Murdock	Willie	24	Wife of James		KY		2		
Moore	Daniel	41		Laborer/Foundry	AL	653 E. Lake	2	Unknown	
Moore	Tina		Wife of Daniel		TN		2		Can't write
Moore	William		Son of Daniel		TN		2		
Moore	Minnie		Daughter of Daniel		TN		2		
Moore	Martha		Daughter of Daniel		TN		2		
Moore	Emma		Daughter of Daniel		TN		2		
Moore	Samuel		Son of Daniel		TN		2		
Matthews	Walter	40		Laborer	GA	653 E. Lake	2	Rent	

1920 Census

Last	First	Age	Relation	Occupation	Born	Address	Ward	Own/Rent	Literacy
Matthews	Lela	34	Wife of Walter	Domestic/Day work	KS		2		
Holbert	Carrie	26			IL	655 E. Lake	2	Rent	
Dickson	Winnie	60	Mother		IL		2		
Ausley	LeRoy	8	Adopted son		IA		2		
Ausley	Dempsey	5	Adopted son		IA		2		
Robinson	Addie	35	Widow	Domestic	OH	655 E. Lake	2	Rent	
Robinson	Elsie	7	Daughter of Addie		IA		2		
Robinson	Georgia	6	Daughter of Addie		IA		2		
Robinson	Carl	5	Nephew of Addie		IA		2		
Edmunds	Morgan	34	Boarder	Laborer/Electric R.R.	GA		2		
Evans	Dorothy	2	Unknown		IA		2		
McCann	Arthur	46		Laborer/Railroad	IL	319 Rosewood	3	Own free	
McCann	Elizabeth	47	Wife of Arthur	Cook/Private family	IL		3		
Miller	James	35	Son-in-law	Cook/Pullman Diner	LA		3		
Miller	Mable	29	Daughter of Arthur	Cleaner/Private family	IL		3		
Miller	Marguerite	4	Granddaughter		IL		3		
Lamar	Ella	62	Widow		VA	301 Rosewood	3	Rent	
Ambrose	Mamie	25	Daughter of Ella/widow	Laundress	IL		3		
Ambrose	Earnest	12	Grandson		IL		3		
Ambrose	May	3	Granddaughter		IL		3		
Barbee	Jasper	24		Cook/Restaurant	TN	291 Rosewood	3	Rent	
Barbee	Ioma	23	Wife of Jasper	Laundress	IN		3		
Morgan	Vera	18	Sister-in-law	Nurse/Private family	IN		3		
[Illegible]	Roger	14	Boarder		IN		3		
Payne	Ada	31	Employed by Charles Dewey	Domestic servant	KY	122 N. Lake	3	Unknown	
Johnson	Fannie	64	Widow	Washwoman	VA	511 Hamilton	3	Own free	
Warren	Phil	40		Boiler man/Gas co.	MO	420 Evans	3	Mortgage	
Warren	Hattie	39	Wife of Phil		MO		3		
Warren	Mabel	12	Daughter of Phil		MO		3		
Warren	John	10	Son of Phil		IL		3		
Warren	Earl	6	Son of Phil		IL		3		
Warren	Elizabeth	1	Daughter of Phil		IL		3		
Wilson	Casander	60	Widow	Laundress at home	Unk.	417 S. Broadway	3		

1920 Census

Last	First	Age	Relation	Occupation	Born	Address	Ward	Own/Rent	Literacy
Morton	John	49		Caterer/Private home	VA	414 Rosewood	3	Own free	
Morton	Frances	44	Wife of John	Caterer/Private home	IA		3		
Morton	Martha	14	Daughter of John		VA		3		
Mayweather	Cornelius	40		Moulder/Iron foundry	OH	401 Rosewood	3	Mortgage	
Mayweather	Emma	41	Wife of Cornelius		KY		3		
Mayweather	Oeida	19	Daughter of Cornelius		IL		3		
Sullivan	Major	23	Son-in-law	Moulder/Foundry	IL		3		
Sullivan	Lawrence	45		Watchman/Iron wks	AL	116 Evans	3	Mortgage	
Metloch	Ada	37	Wife of Lawrence		TN		3		
Metloch	William	62		Laborer/Electric plant	TN	340 Talma	3	Mortgage	Can't write
Catlett	Eliza	68	Wife of William		VA		3		Illiterate
Catlett	Mary	46	Daughter of William		TN		3		
Richerson	Charles	49		Laborer/Dry goods store	MI	473 Jackson	3	Own free	
Dyer	Alberta	48	Wife of Charles		MI		3		
Dyer	Arietta	17	Daughter of Charles		IL		3		
Dyer	Adelia	60	Mother-in-law (widow)		MD		3		
Rausch	William	Unk.		Teamster/City	Unk.	793 Fifth Ave.	3	Own	Illiterate
Edwards	Caroline	78	Housekeeper	Domestic servant	TN		3		Illiterate
Jackson	Owen	31		Laborer/Railroad	IL	795 Fifth Ave.	3	Rent	
White	Leahla	26	Wife of Owen		IL		3		
White	John	6	Son of Owen		IL		3		
White	Jean	3	Daughter of Owen		IL		3		
White	Richard	20	Boarder	Laborer/Railroad	KY		3		
Graham	George	42		Boiler washer/R.R.	TN	599 Binder	3	Mortgage	
Greer	Lola	40	Wife of George (white)		TN		3		
Greer	Claude	18	Step-son (white)	Laborer/confectionery	IL		3		
Greer	Myrite	16	Step-daughter (white)		IL		3		
Greer	Samela	13	Step-daughter (white)		IL		3		
Greer	George	8	Son of George		IL		3		
Greer	Carl	5	Son of George		IL		3		
Greer	Orval	1	Son of George		IL		3		
Washington	Willis	49		Machine operator	MO	563 North Ave	3	Rent	
Washington	Cordelia	39	Wife of Willis		TN		3		

1920 Census

Last	First	Age	Relation	Occupation	Born	Address	Ward	Own/Rent	Literacy
Washington	Florence	16	Daughter of Willis		IL		3		
Washington	Frances	14	Son of Willis		IL		3		
Washington	Dorothy	5	Daughter of Willis		IL		3		
Washington	Catherine	3	Daughter of Willis		IL		3		
Lewis	Edward	36		Laborer/Car shop	IL	672 Fifth Ave.	3	Rent	
Lewis	Blanche	29	Wife of Edward	Cook/Club house	KY		3		
[Illegible]	Lizzie	42	Listed with Harry Coats	Maid/Housekeeper	AL	76 Lincoln	4	Unk.	
McCann	[Illegible]	Unk.	Wife of O.	Miner/Coal mine	IA	162 S. Broadway	4	Rent	
McCann	Gertrude	Unk.	Wife of O.		MO		4		
McCann	Samuel	Unk.	Son of O.		IL		4		
Shively	Edward	36		Hod carrier	KY	152 S. Broadway	4	Rent	
Shively	Cora	31	Wife of Edward		FL		4		Illiterate
Shively	Frank	7	Son of Edward		IL		4		
Shively	[Illegible]	5 mo.	Daughter of Edward		IL		4		
Carter	Elizabeth	43	Widow	Housework	IN	152 S. Broadway	4	Rent	
Carter	Elizabeth	10	Daughter of Elizabeth		IL		4		
Holdman	David	19	Boarder	Laborer/Shop yard	MS		4		
Allen	Joe	45	Boarder	Laborer/Shop yard	FL		4		
Warren	William	46	Boarder	Waiter	IL		4		
Andrews	Lulu	32	Boarder/Widow	Cook/Restaurant	TX		4		
Bradford	Andrew	55	Widower	Hod carrier	MS	111 Benton	4	Rent	Illiterate
Bradford	Carl	18	Son of Andrew	Laborer/Steel plant	IL		4		
Scott	George	35	Boarder (married)	Laborer/Building	MO		4		
Ivey	Albert	44	Boarder	Laborer/Building	IL		4		
Bassett	Rufus	36		Hod carrier	MO	114 Stone Ave	4	Rent	
Bassett	Ollie	34	Wife of Rufus	Waitress/Restaurant	IL		4		
Williams	William	49	Boarder	Laborer/Foundry	TN		4		
Crenshaw	Normal	32	Employed by Solemnus Seamans	Domestic servant	KY	15 S. East Ave	4	Unk.	
Washington	Hattie	70	Widow		TN	695 North Ave	4	Rent	
Boyd	Nathan	47		Porter	IA	643 Second Ave	4	Mortgage	
Boyd	Sarah	47	Wife of Nathan		TN		4		
Miller	Wilhelmeta	5	Granddaughter		IL		4		
Williams	James	50		Teamster	VA	643 Second Ave	4	Rent	

1920 Census

Last	First	Age	Relation	Occupation	Born	Address	Ward	Own/Rent	Literacy
Williams	Julia	41	Wife of James		VA	139 Main St.	4	Unk.	
Carlisle	Louis	32		Laborer/rail yards	KY		5		
Carlisle	Surento	21	Wife of Louis	Odd jobs/Private family	IN		5		
Taylor	Jerry	50		Proprietor of bakery	KS	68 N. Broadway	5	Rent	
Taylor	Beatrice	48	Wife of Jerry	Assistant/Bakery	IL		5		
Chatman	Rosa	36	Widow	Keeps rooming house	MS	109 Spring	5	Rent	
Cason	Thomas	49	Boarder	Laborer/Round house	KY		5		
Walsh	Roy	19	Boarder	Laborer/Factory	IL		5		
Well	Philip	22	Boarder	Laborer/Coal yards	TX		5		
Jordan	William	42		Janitor/Round house	IL	113 Spring	5	Rent	
Jordan	Anna	26	Wife of William		MS		5		
Spriggs	Catherine	48		Keeps boarding house	IL	58 N. Lincoln	5	Rent	
Spriggs	John	78	Father-in-law		TN		5		
Edwards	Fred	44	Boarder	Drives/Town	IL		5		
Jackson	Raymond	20	Boarder	Laborer	IL		5		
Patton	Tom	35	Boarder	Laborer	OK		5		
Hatchet	McDonald	17	Boarder	Laborer	KY		5		
Bridget	Clifford	38	Boarder	Hair dresser	KY		5		
Roberts	Rosa	56	Boarder		IL		5		
Bowdas	Pete	49	Boarder	Laborer	KS		5		
Johnson	Lewis	58		Boiler maker/CB&Q	NC	570 Benton	5	Own free	
Johnson	Daisy	41	Wife of Lewis		IN		5		
[Illegible]	William	13	Step-son		IL		5		
Johnson	Daniel	23		Laborer/Well works	IL	570 Benton	5	Rent	
Johnson	Esther	21	Wife of Daniel	Sewing	IL		5		
Webb	Hugh	35		Janitor/Social club	KY	21 S. East Ave.	5	Mortgage	
Webb	Hazel	33	Wife of Hugh	Cook/Social club	IL		5		
Webb	Vera	8	Daughter of Hugh		IL		5		
Crenshaw	Arthur	47		Laborer/Car shops	MO	15 S. East Ave.	5	Rent	
Crowler	Mollie	65	Mother-in-law		MO		5		Illiterate
Farmer	Lorie	20	Half-sister	Servant/Private family	MO		5		
Ousley	William	49		Laborer/Car shops	KY	11 S. East Ave.	5	Rent	
Ousley	Mamie	47	Wife of William		AL		5		Illiterate

181

1920 Census

Last	First	Age	Relation	Occupation	Born	Address	Ward	Own/Rent	Literacy
Patterson	John	49		Laborer/Railroad	WI	11 S. East Ave.	5	Rent	
Patterson	Claudie	46	Wife of John	Servant/Private family	IN		5		
Crumwell	Benjamin	19	Boarder	Laborer/Cooperage	AL		5		
Bell	John H.	55		Minister/A. M. E.	KY	543 Main St.	5	Rent	
Bell	Minola	52	Wife of John		IN		5		
Bell	[Illegible]	13	Daughter of John		IA		5		
White	Frank	55		Janitor/Theatre	IL	22 Rose	5	Rent	
White	Jennie	52	Wife of Frank	Servant/Private family	IL		5		
White	Dorthy	19	Daughter of Frank		IL		5		
White	Louis	16	Son of Frank	Elevator operator	IL		5		
White	Leonard	15	Son of Frank	Janitor/Theatre	IL		5		
Artis	George	63	Boarder	Teamster/Flour mill	IL		5		
Smith	Ferdinand	37		Janitor/Furniture store	IL	26 Rose	5	Mortgage	
Smith	Carrie	28	Wife of Ferdinand		WI		5		
Smith	Harold	5	Son of Ferdinand		IL		5		
Smith	Doris	3	Daughter of Ferdinand		IL		5		
Smith	James	1	Son of Ferdinand		IL		5		
Moore	William	49		Chauffeur/delivery truck	TN	16 S. East Ave.	5	Mortgage	
Moore	Adelaide	25	Daughter of William	Store keeper/Grocery	IL		5		
Mills	Dewey	23	Boarder	Chauffeur/Lumber co.	NC		5		
Mills	Thomas	26	Boarder	Electrician/Garage	NC		5		
Hoard	Ella	25	Listed with William Fowler	Domestic servant	MI	621 Main St.	5	Unknown	
Matthews	Jane	54		Laundress	IL	795 Grand	5	Rent	
Hamlet	Louis	28	Son of Jane	Cooper/Cooperage	IL		5		
Douglas	Edward	55	Wife of Edward	Moulder/Iron works	VA	95 Sumner	5	Mortgage	
Douglas	Catherine	53	Wife of Edward		TN		5		
Douglas	Ralph	23	Son of Edward	Laborer/Factory	IL		5		
Douglas	Alma	21	Daughter-in-law	Domestic servant	KY		5		
Cooper	John	23	Boarder	Laborer/Factory	IL		5		
Barbee	Charles	39		Laborer/coal	KY	845 Grand	5	Mortgage	
Barbee	Maggie	34	Wife of Charles	Laundress	KY		5		
Barbee	Courtland	14	Son of Charles	Student	KY		5		
Barbee	Ruth	12	Daughter of Charles	Student	IL		5		

182

1920 Census

Last	First	Age	Relation	Occupation	Born	Address	Ward	Own/Rent	Literacy
Barbee	Thomas	10	Son of Charles	Student	IL		5		
Hilliard	William	48		Janitor/Factory	IL	Farnsworth	5	Mortgage	
Hilliard	Nellie	49	Wife of William	Laundress	IL		5		
Hilliard	William	13	Son of William	Student	IL		5		
Hilliard	Anna	83	Mother of William		KY		5		
Reiley	Charles	40	Son-in-law	Chauffeur/Coal co.	MO		5		
Reiley	Alice	26	Daughter of William	Laundress	IL		5		
Reiley	Charles	2	Grandson		ND		5		
Reiley	Dorothy	7	Granddaughter	Student	IL		5		
Patterson	John	33		Teamster	KY	830 Grand	5	Mortgage	
Patterson	Carrie	30	Wife of John		KY		5		
Patterson	Mary	9	Daughter of John	Student	IL		5		
Patterson	Allenette	8	Daughter of John	Student	IL		5		
Patterson	William	7	Son of John	Student	IL		5		
Patterson	LaValle	4	Son of John		IL		5		
Patterson	Russell	2	Son of John		IL		5		
Scott	George	42		Laborer/Cabinet fcty	KY	61 Kendall	5	Rent	
Scott	Nancy	42	Wife of George		KY		5		
Scott	Ward	21	Son of George	Laborer/Iron foundry	IL		5		
Scott	Pauline	18	Daughter of George	Domestic servant	IL		5		
Scott	Elmer	16	Son of George	Truck boy/Stove works	IL		5		
Scott	Delos	11	Son of George	Student	IL		5		
Scott	James	8	Son of George	Student	IL		5		
Scott	Naoma	6	Daughter of George	Student	IL		5		
Scott	Jean	2	Daughter of George		IL		5		
Scott	David	1	Son of George		IL		5		
Harris	Goldie	35		Keeps boarding house	IL	135 N. Lincoln	6	Rent	
Pickett	LeRoy	23	Boarder	Waiter at hotel	IA		6		
Pickett	Eva	18	Wife of LeRoy		MO		6		
Williams	Saphria	26	Boarder	Laborer/Coal yards	MO		6		Illiterate
Williams	Helen	28	Wife of Saphria		IL		6		
Atchey	George	37	Boarder	Laborer/Railroad	VA		6		
Cyrus	William	37	Boarder	Waiter at hotel	MI		6		

183

1920 Census

Last	First	Age	Relation	Occupation	Born	Address	Ward	Own/Rent	Literacy
Moulden	Daniel	43	Boarder (married)	Waiter at hotel	IL		6		
Williams	Robert	21	Boarder	Waiter at hotel	TN		6		
Rollis	Jay	48	Boarder	Vaudeville actor	MD		6		
Scheffey	Wade	46		Head waiter at hotel	VA	167 N. Lincoln	6	Rent	
Scheffey	Leopolde	35	Wife of Wade		WV		6		
Scheffey	Kathleen	14	Daughter of Wade	Student	WV		6		
Scheffey	Julia	8	Daughter of Wade	Student	WV		6		
Morris	Clarence	18	Boarder	Waiter at hotel	IN		6		
Henry	Harry	19	Boarder	Waiter at hotel	TN		6		
Russell	Albert	24	Boarder	Waiter at hotel	IN		6		
Daniel	William	37	Boarder	Waiter at hotel	KY		6		
Bailey	Edward	35	Boarder	Waiter at hotel	KY		6		
Bolton	Lin	42		Laborer/Railroad	TN	136 N. Broadway	6	Rent	
Bolton	Sarah	40	Wife of Lin		TN		6		
Airington	Joana	31	Sister-in-law		TN		6		
Airington	Lee	24	Brother-in-law	Laborer/Chemical works	KY		6		
King	William	41		Porter/Railroad	GA	136 N. Broadway	6	Rent	
King	Laura	35	Wife of William		TN		6		
Allen	Clarence	22	Boarder	Laborer/Electric R. R.	IL		6		
Allen	Goldie	21	Wife of Clarence		IL		6		
Allen	Russell	3			IL		6		
Taylor	William	64		Laborer/Electric R.R.	MO	142 N. Broadway	6	Rent	Illiterate
Taylor	Jennie	62	Wife of William	Laundress	Canada		6		Illiterate
Taylor	William	7	Son of William	Student	IL		6		
Taylor	Earl	26	Son		IL		6		
Wash	Eva	25	Daughter of William	Cook/restaurant	IL		6		
Wash	Katherine	6	Granddaughter		IL		6		
Wash	Albert	7	Grandson		IL		6		
Medbank	William	23	Boarder	Porter/restaurant	GA		6		
Blackman	Mary	73	Mother-in-law		MS		6		
Morris	William	37		Laborer	IL	142 N. Broadway	6	Rent	
Morris	Bertha	35	Wife of William		MO		6		
Carlyle	Tyler	35	Boarder	Laborer/garage	IL		6		

1920 Census

Last	First	Age	Relation	Occupation	Born	Address	Ward	Own/Rent	Literacy
Aust	Pearl	42	Widow	Washing	IN	148 N. Broadway	6	Rent	
Cleveland	Jerry	24	Son of Pearl	Laborer/railroad	AR		6		
Johnigan	Henry	29		Laborer/meat company	IL	150 N. Broadway	6	Unk	
Johnigan	Pearl	29	Wife of Henry		IL		6		
Monroe	Claude	24	Boarder	Waiter at hotel	IL		6		
Randall	Charlie	31		Waitress at hotel	KY	160 N. Broadway	6	Rent	
Thomason	Will	42	Boarder	Laborer/stock yards	MO		6		
Airington	Lee	24	Boarder	Laborer/chemical co.	KY		6		
Schmidt	Lora	48			GA	164 N. Broadway	6	Rent	
Davis	William	35	Boarder	Laborer/machine shop	AL		6		
Smith	Sadie	30	Boarder	Waitress/restaurant	MI		6		
Hill	Jay	30		Laborer/railroad	MS	168 N. Broadway	6	Rent	
Hill	Velma	25	Wife of Jay		KY		6		
Smith	Frankie	37			KY	172 N. Broadway	6	Rent	
Franklin	Elisha	36	Boarder	Laborer/machine shop	AR		6		
Woods	Robert	26		Laborer/foundry	IL	174 N. Broadway	6	Rent	
Woods	Flossie	23	Wife of Robert		IL		6		
Woods	Geraldine	2	Daughter of Robert		IL		6		
Hays	Robert	36		Barber shop	IN	190 N. Broadway	6	Rent	
Hays	Amanda	41	Wife of Robert		KY		6		
Hays	Sadie	24	Step-daughter	Housework	KY		6		
Hays	Mary	2	Daughter of Robert		IL		6		
Blackburn	Jim	26	Boarder	Laborer/railroad	IL		6		
Blackburn	Mattie	25	Wife of Jim		IL		6		
Willis	William	61	Boarder (widower)		KY		6		Illiterate
Jenkins	George	35		Tailor at home	AL	194 N. Broadway	6	Mortgage	
Jenkins	Margaret	27	Wife of George		IL		6		
Baine	Marshall	27	Boarder (divorced)	Chauffer/garage	GA		6		
Perkins	Elizabeth	45	Housework		KY	198 N. Broadway	6	Rent	
Franklin	Althea	68	Widow	Keeps boarding house	AL	200 N. Broadway	6	Mortgage	Can't read
Wilson	Charlie	36	Boarder	Waiter/soft drinks	MO		6		
Parker	William	65	Boarder	Janitor/building	MO		6		Illiterate
Robinson	George	25	Boarder	Laborer/shop yards	MO		6		

185

1920 Census

Last	First	Age	Relation	Occupation	Born	Address	Ward	Own/Rent	Literacy
Marshall	Albert	23	Boarder	Laborer/foundry	KS	204 N. Broadway	6		
Jackson	Tom	52		Laborer/foundry	KY		6	Mortgage	
Thomas	Mamie	30	Housekeeper (widow)	Domestic	IN		6		
Porter	William	23		Laborer/foundry	KS	212 N. Broadway	6	Mortgage	
Porter	Blanche	33	Wife of William		IL		6		
Hardin	James	20	Boarder	Laborer/railroad	GA		6		
Boger	Calvin	73	Widower	Bricklayer	GA	228 Claim St.	6	Own	
Elder	George	26		Waiter at hotel	IL	189 Lincoln	6	Rent	
Elder	Maude	29	Wife of George		MO		6		
Weaver	Charles	26	Boarder	Porter on dining car	MO		6		
Weaver	Mary	20	Wife of Charles		MO		6		
Lewis	Alfred	26		Craneman/foundry	TX	150 Broadway	6	Rent	
Lewis	Nancy	37	Wife of Alfred		IL		6		
Reel	Ethel	16	Daughter		IL		6		
Reel	Carol	15	Daughter		IL		6		
Reel	Wilbur	13	Son	Student	IL		6		
Mitchell	Pearl	31		Keeps boarding house	IA	170 Broadway	6	Rent	
Haggert	John	Unk	Boarder	Laborer	IL		6		
Thomas	Joseph	31		Laborer/cotton mill	IL	170 Broadway	6	Rent	
Thomas	Emma	27	Wife of Joseph		OH		6		
Travis	William	38		Craneman/machine shop	KY	208 N. Root	6	Rent	
Travis	Daisy	31	Wife of William	Housework	KY		6		
Brown	Clara	52	Widow		NY	163 N. Root	6	Rent	
Madison	Arin	9	Grandson	Student	IL		6		
Bell	John	52	Widower	Fireman/well works	KY	165 N. Root	6	Rent	
Bell	Elayne	12	Daughter of John	Student	IL		6		
West	Bert	32		Moulder/foundry	KS	167 N. Root	6	Rent	
West	Novela	25	Wife of Bert		NC		6		
West	Bertie	1	Daughter of Bert		IL		6		
Long	Samuel	52		Laborer	AL	266 College	6	Mortgage	
Long	Sarah	50	Wife of Samuel	Dress maker at home	IL		6		
Long	Martha	14	Daughter of Samuel		IL		6		
Marshall	Lidia	76	Mother-in-law (widow)		AL		6		

1920 Census

Last	First	Age	Relation	Occupation	Born	Address	Ward	Own/Rent	Literacy
Kirkland	Lucy	24	Boarder	Laborer/mfg. co.	AR		6		
Jameson	Robert	19	Boarder	Laborer/railroad	MS		6		
LaMar	Theodore	18	Boarder	Laborer/restaurant	IL		6		
Frazier	Henry	39		Paver (unemployed)	KY	266 College	6	Rent	
Frazier	Henrietta	34	Wife of Henry		IN		6		
Franklin	Bulah	38	Widow	Domestic servant	GA	116 Indiana	6	Rent	
Franklin	Edward	8	Son of Bulah	Student	IL		6		
Dixon	Winnie	56	Boarder (widow)	Domestic servant	ME		6		
Dixon	Louise	38	Boarder	Domestic servant	IL		6		
Hudson	James	54		Chiropodist	Unk	118 Indiana	6	Mortgage	
Hudson	Emma	65	Wife of James		AL		6		
Walsh	Thomas	12	Boarder	Student	IL		6		
Carter	Albert	28	Boarder	Welder	IA		6		
Alberts	George	40	Boarder	Laborer	OK		6		Illiterate
Simmons	Edwin	39		Cook/club room	IL	631 Kane	6	Rent	
Simmons	Anna	33	Wife of Edwin		IL		6		
Simmons	Violet	12	Daughter of Edwin	Student	IL		6		
Simmons	Edwin	10	Son of Edwin	Student	IL		6		
Simmons	Maxine	9	Daughter of Edwin	Student	IL		6		
Simmons	Constance	6	Daughter of Edwin	Student	IL		6		
Simmons	Waneta	4	Daughter of Edwin		IL		6		
Simmons	Albert	1	Son of Edwin		IL		6		
Pervine	Arthur	36		Laborer/iron foundry	TN	601 Kane St.	6	Rent	Illiterate
Pervine	Katherine	33	Wife of Arthur		IL		6		
Thomas	Louis	37		Janitor/stove works	MS	876 New York	6	Rent	
Thomas	Lettie	27	Wife of Louis	Laundress	IL		6		
Thomas	Geraldine	6	Daughter of Louis	Student	IL		6		
Moore	Elizabeth	69	Widow		TN	655 Kane St.	6	Mortgage	Illiterate
Moore	James	42	Son of Elizabeth	House construction	TN		6		
Moore	Bessie	36	Daughter of Elizabeth		IL		6		
Moore	Howard	15	Grandson of Elizabeth	Student	IL		6		
Bell	James	39		Fireman/gas company	TN	121 Indiana	6	Rent	Illiterate
Bell	Lula	39	Wife of James	Laundress	IL		6		

187

1920 Census

Last	First	Age	Relation	Occupation	Born	Address	Ward	Own/Rent	Literacy
Bell	Arthur	11	Son of James	Student	IL		6		
Catlett	George	52		Laborer/gas company	TN	115 Indiana	6	Mortgage	
Catlett	Rosa	42	Wife of George	Laborer/private family	IL		6		
Catlett	Albert	6	Son of George	Student	IL		6		
Watson	Charles	53		Laborer/railroad	MO	423 Kane St.	6	Mortgage	
Watson	Bessie	47	Wife of Charles		MO		6		
Watson	Ruth	16	Daughter of Charles	Machine operator	IA		6		
Watson	Marie	13	Daughter of Charles	Student	IL		6		
Watson	Earnest	7	Son of Charles	Student	IL		6		
Muse	Josephine	Unk	Widow		TN	396 Kane St.	6	Rent	Can't write
Muse	Earnest	Unk	Son of Josephine (married)	Painter [City Directory]	TN		6		
Muse	Clarence	Unk	Son of Josephine (divorced)	[possibly same as Earnest]	IL		6	
Wilson	Stanford	50		Janitor/restaurant	IL	400 Kane St.	6	Own	
Wilson	Aurelia	32			KS		6		
Mitchell	Louise	66	Sister of Stanford (widow)		IL		6		
Grahm	Robert	35		Cook/boarding house	KY	432 Kane St.	6	Rent	
Grahm	Nellie	34	Wife of Robert		KY		6		
Grahm	Lerlien	16	Daughter of Robert	Domestic servant	KY		6		
Grahm	Mary	11	Daughter of Robert	Student	KY		6		
Grahm	James	8	Son of Robert	Student	KY		6		
Grahm	William	4	Son of Robert		KY		6		
VanTrees	Henry	27	Nephew	Laborer/tool factory	KY		6		
Samson	John	46		Laborer/iron foundry	MO	432 Kane St.	6	Rent	
Samson	Ellie	36			KY		6		
Samson	Olla	17	Step-daughter	Seamstress/apron fcty.	KY		6		
Samson	[Illegible]	19	Step-daughter (married)		KY		6		
Samson	Jane	2	Step-granddaughter		IN		6		
Simpson	Josie	30	Niece (married)	Seamstress/apron fcty.	IN		6		
Simpson	Margaret	10	Grandniece	Student	KY		6		
Hall	Elisha	64		Janitor/office building	IL	231 Beach	6	Mortgage	
Hall	Isabella	50	Wife of Elisha	Dress maker at home	IL		6		
Washington	Mary	72	Mother-in-law (widow)		AL		6		Illiterate

1920 Census

Last	First	Age	Relation	Occupation	Born	Address	Ward	Own/Rent	Literacy
Watson	Charles	46		Chauffer/private family	IA	551 Kane St.	6	Rent	
Watson	Oneida	35	Wife of Charles	Domestic servant	IA		6		
Watson	Beatrice	15	Daughter of Charles	Student	IL		6		
Watson	Charlie	12	Son of Charles	Student	IA		6		
Watson	Ruth	10	Daughter of Charles	Student	IL		6		
Greer	Martha	60	Widow	Laundress at home	TN	565 Kane St.	6	Mortgage	
Greer	Soloman	35	Son of Martha (married)	Laborer/pump factory	TN		6		
Greer	Theodus	21	Son of Martha		TN		6		Illiterate
Greer	Walter	20	Son of Martha	Laborer/tool factory	TN		6		
Allen	Grant	30		Chauffer/coal company	IL	569 Kane St.	6	Mortgage	
Allen	Cora	28	Wife of Grant	Domestic servant	IL		6		
Brown	James	35		Works in car shops	TN	571 Kane St.	6	Mortgage	
Brown	Mary	34	Wife of James		IL		6		
Brown	Cary	7	Son of James	Student	IL		6		
Brown	Arien	4	Daughter of James		IL		6		
Spriggs	Elenor	41	Widow	Machine operator	IL	573 Kane St.	6	Rent	
Spriggs	William	22	Son of Elenor		VA		6		
Spriggs	Norman	15	Son of Elenor		IL		6		Illiterate
Powell	Hanah	70	Mother of Elenor (widow)		AL		6		Illiterate
Carter	Elza	33		Laborer/box factory	IL	112 N. Ohio	6	Own	
Carter	Leora	31	Wife of Elza		IL		6		
Smith	Henry	54		Janitor/theatre	IL	114 N. Ohio	6	Mortgage	
Smith	Margaret	48	Wife of Henry		IL		6		
Smith	Amelia	21	Daughter of Henry	Machine operator	IL		6		
Smith	Camilla	15	Daughter of Henry	Student	IL		6		
Smith	Merle	12	Son of Henry	Student	IL		6		
Smith	Marion	7	Daughter of Henry	Student	IL		6		
Smith	Fredrick	4	Son of Henry		IL		6		
Perkins	Charles	23		Janitor/office building	TX	151 N. Ohio	6	Rent	
Perkins	Mildred	21	Wife of Charles		IL		6		
Perkins	Junior	1	Son of Charles		IL		6		
Jackson	William	45		Laborer/odd jobs	LA	588 Kane St.	6	Mortgage	Illiterate
Jackson	Mary	48	Wife of William	Domestic servant	VA		6		Illiterate

1920 Census

Last	First	Age	Relation	Occupation	Born	Address	Ward	Own/Rent	Literacy
Chambers	Charles	45		Laborer/electric co.	KY	588 Kane St.	6		
Chambers	Ossie	57	Wife of Charles	Laundress	KY		6		
Douglas	Edward	28		Laborer/garage	IL	588 Kane St.	6	Rent	
Douglas	Marie	26	Wife of Edward		IL		6		
Douglas	Katherine	3	Daughter of Edward		IL		6		
Coleman	Garfield	39	Married	Laborer/pump factory	MS	624 Kane St.	6	Rent	Illiterate
Coleman	[Illegible]	15	Son of Garfield	Student	MS		6		
Coleman	John	9	Son of Garfield	Student	MS		6		
Gibson	George	42		Janitor/building	LA	632 Kane St.	6	Mortgage	
Gibson	[Illegible]	35	Wife of George	Domestic servant	MS		6		
Johnson	Louis	50	Boarder	Farm laborer	LA		6		
Johnson	Mary	46	Wife of Louis		LA		6		
Johnson	James	21	Son of Louis	Laborer in hotel	LA		6		
Johnson	Josiah	19	Son of Louis	Laborer/tool factory	LA		6		
Smith	Mamie	26	Boarder (married)	Domestic servant	LA		6		
Poplus	Gilbert	27	Boarder	Laborer in hotel	LA		6		
Carter	Charles	69		Laborer/odd jobs	OH	160 Indiana	6	Own	
Carter	Rosa	60	Wife of Charles		IL		6		
Irving	William	48		Laborer/gas company	KS	798 Pond	6	Rent	
Irving	Louisa	38	Wife of William		MO		6		
Howard	Henry	38		Laborer/street railway	MO	794 Pond	6	Rent	
Howard	Annie	26	Wife of Henry		TX		6		
Crytchfield	A.	7	Step-son	Student	TX		6		
Grier	Andrew	36		Machine operator	IL	244 Farnsworth	6	Mortgage	
Grier	Rose	35	Wife of Andrew	Laundress	IL		6		
Duke	Matthew	54	Widow	Laborer/job work	TN	201 Trask St.	6	Rent	
Duke	LeRoy	27	Son of Matthew	Laborer	IL		6		
Duke	Amos	24	Son of Matthew	Laborer	IL		6		
Duke	Ernest	20	Son of Matthew	Chauffer	IL		6		
Duke	Mildred	17	Daughter of Matthew		IL		6		
Duke	Lilla	16	Daughter of Matthew		IL		6		
Williams	Laura	Unk	Widow		TN	181 Indiana	6	Own	
Williams	Adra	Unk	Daughter of Laura	Private music teacher	IL		6		

1920 Census

Last	First	Age	Relation	Occupation	Born	Address	Ward	Own/Rent	Literacy
Williams	Arthur	Unk	Son of Laura (divorced)	Porter/barber shop	IL		6		
Meadows	May	43	Widow	Laundress	IL	161 Indiana	6	Rent	
Meadows	Arnold	16	Son of May	Laborer/cooperage	IL		6		
Meadows	Barbra	12	Daughter of May	Student	IL		6		
Meadows	May	9	Daughter of May		IL		6		
Franklin	Leonard	40	Boarder	Laborer/hardware mfr	MO		6		
Graves	Eli	48		Laborer/iron foundry	MS	161 Indiana	6	Rent	
Graves	Margaret	40	Wife of Eli		MS		6		
Graves	Joseph	14	Son of Eli	Student	MS		6		
Smith	William	56		Laborer/iron foundry	KY	155 Indiana	6	Mortgage	
Smith	Eliza	42	Wife of William		KY		6		
Hopson	Myra	70	Mother-in-law (widow)		KY		6		Illiterate
Hopson	Mabel	16	Niece		KY		6		Illiterate
Brown	Ruth	14	Niece	Student	IL		6		
Carter	Isaac	34		Stone mason/contractor	TN	673 Fenton	6	Own	
Carter	Madora	34	Wife of Isaac	Laundress	IL		6		
Williams	David	44		Laborer/paint factory	IL	679 Pond	6	Own	
Williams	Clara	36	Wife of David	Waitress in hotel	IL		6		
Williams	Donald	17	Son of David	Student	IL		6		
Williams	Kenneth	13	Son of David	Student	MS		6		
Warren	Edward	68	Father-in-law (widow)	Laborer/car shops	FL		6		Illiterate
Fonzey	James	43		Fireman/car shops	IA	656 Kane St.	6	Rent	
Fonzey	Roxey	40	Wife of James		IA		6		
Fonzey	Luellen	14	Daughter of James	Student	IA		6		
Fonzey	Dorothy	10	Daughter of James	Student	IL		6		
Harding	Edward	44		[illegible]	Poland	652 Kane	6	Mortgage	
Harding	Martha	38	Wife of Edward	Office maid	IL		6		
Harding	Elizabeth	17	Daughter of Edward	Student	IL		6		
Harding	Helen	9	Daughter of Edward		IL		6		
Harding	Julia	5	Daughter of Edward		IL		6		
Harding	Anna	3	Daughter of Edward		IL		6		
Alexander	Joseph	26		Helper/foundry	OK	287 N. Root	7	Rent	
Alexander	Pearl	20	Wife of Joseph		MO		7		

191

1920 Census

Last	First	Age	Relation	Occupation	Born	Address	Ward	Own/Rent	Literacy
White	Clyde	17	Brother-in-law	Helper/factory	OK	176 Superior	7	Rent	
Humbles	John	31		Laborer/electric co.	VA		7		
Humbles	Estella	30	Wife of John		IN		7		
Humbles	Charles	10	Son of John	Student	IN		7		
Taylor	Charles	34		Laborer	MO	174 Superior	7	Rent	
Taylor	Corrine	32	Wife of Charles		MO		7		
Bowman	Henry	8	Son	Student	MO		7		
Williams	Martha	80	Grandmother (widow)		KY		7		
Jones	Bernard	30		Teamster	MD	287 N. Root	7	Rent	
Jones	Bertha	30	Wife of Bernard	Housework	VA		7		
Vaughn	Thomas	54		Teamster	VA	197 Superior	7	Rent	
Vaughn	Carrie	55	Wife of Thomas		VA		7		
Brown	John	25		Laborer/foundry	IL	274 Beach	7	Rent	
Brown	Mattie	28	Wife of John		KY		7		
McCann	Katharine	13	Step-daughter	Student	IL		7		
Carlisle	Thomas	59	Father-in-law (widow)		KY		7		
Gates	Frank	53		Janitor/well works	MO	272 Beach	7	Rent	Illiterate
Gates	Laura	60	Wife of Frank	Seamstress at home	NB		7		
Lewis	Harry	43		Tailor shop	MO	274 Superior	7	Mortgage	
Lewis	Anna	41	Wife of Harry		KS		7		
Lewis	Elbert	12	Son of Harry	Student	NB		7		
Lewis	Harry	11	Son of Harry	Student	NB		7		
Lewis	Velma	9	Daughter of Harry	Student	IL		7		
Lewis	Anna May	8	Daughter of Harry	Student	IL		7		
Lewis	Willard	6	Son of Harry	Student	IL		7		
Adams	Clifford	30		Laborer/gas company	IL	314 Beach	7	Mortgage	
Adams	Ada	29	Wife of Clifford		IL		7		
Dishman	Ida	28	Sister (divorced)	Housework	IL		7		
Dishman	Genevieve	8	Niece	Student	IL		7		
Campbell	Claude	33	Boarder (married)	Waiter at hotel	IL		7		
Reese	Arthur	28		Barber shop	IL	312 Beach	7	Rent	
Reese	Addie	26	Wife of Arthur		KY		7		
Reese	Lucille	6	Daughter of Arthur	Student	KS		7		

1920 Census

Last	First	Age	Relation	Occupation	Born	Address	Ward	Own/Rent	Literacy
Reese	[Illegible]	5	Daughter of Arthur	Student	KS		7		
Reese	Lillian	1	Daughter of Arthur		IL		7		
Reese	Arthur	5 mo	Son of Arthur		IL		7		
Gailes	Benjamin	34		Minister	MS	312 Beach	7	Rent	
Gailes	Lilly	35	Wife of Benjamin		GA		7		
Cooper	Thomas	79		Gardener [City Directory]	VA	715 Sheridan	7	Mortgage	
Cooper	Lucy	58	Wife of Thomas		MS		7		
Cooper	Daisy	34	Daughter of Thomas	Maker/wrapper mfr.	IL		7		
Cooper	Paul	37	Son of Thomas	Mechanic/foundry	IL		7		
Seals	Carson	34		Laborer/works out	MO	276 N. Broadway	Unk.	Rent	
Seals	Grace	32	Wife of Carson		MO		Unk.		
Hazard	Norton	Unk		Unk	Unk	274 Beach	Unk.	Unk	

End Notes

Introduction

[1] R. Waite Joslyn and Frank W. Joslyn, <u>History of Kane County, Illinois, Vol. I</u> (Chicago: The Pioneer Publishing Co., 1908), 5.
[2] Ibid.

Chapter 1, The Dawn of a City

[3] Vernon Derry, <u>Aurora, In the Beginning</u> (Aurora, IL: The Kelmscott Press, 1963), 11.
[4] Ibid., 11.
[5] Ibid., 12.
[6] Ibid., 14.
[7] Jean O'Brien, "A Study of Aurora Schools, 1835-1935" (Masters thesis: Northern Illinois University, 1990), 13.
[8] Ibid., 13.
[9] Derry, <u>Aurora, In the Beginning</u>, 17.
[10] Susan Palmer, "Building Ethnic Communities in a Small City: Romanians and Mexicans in Aurora, Illinois, 1900-1940" (Ph.D. Diss., Northern Illinois University, 1986), 21.
[11] O'Brien, 13.
[12] "City Charter: An Act to Incorporate the City of Aurora, and the Establish and Inferior Court Therein," in <u>The Charter and Ordinances of the City of Aurora (To June 1, 1863, Inclusive), Together With the Acts of the General Assembly Relating to the City, and Other Miscellaneous Acts</u>, comp. A. G. M'Dole (Aurora, IL: Bangs and Knickerbocker, 1863), 26-27, 36; "Aurora Served by 46 Mayors Since The First, B. F. Hall, Took Office in 1872," <u>Aurora Beacon News</u>, 5 September 1937, sec. 3, p. 4.
[13] Palmer, 22.
[14] <u>Federal Writers Project</u>, Illinois: A Descriptive and Historical Guide (Chicago: A. C. McClurg & Co., 1939), 158.
[15] Palmer, 24.
[16] Palmer, 13.
[17] Charles S. Battle, ed., <u>Centennial Biographical and Historical Record of Aurora for One Hundred Years, 1837-1937 and the Chicago, Burlington & Quincy Railroad for Eighty-Six Years, 1850-1937</u> (1937), 35.
[18] Milton Gordon, <u>Assimilation in American Life: The Role of Race, Religion and National Origins</u> (New York: Oxford University Press, 1964), 5.
[19] Palmer, 26.
[20] <u>City Directory of Aurora, 1890-93</u> (Aurora, IL: Knickerbocker & Hodder, 1890), 65-66.
[21] <u>Aurora As It Is, First Annual Gazetteer and Directory of the City of Aurora, Ill.</u> (Aurora, IL: Knickerbocker and Hodder, 1868), 54; Advertisement, <u>Aurora Beacon</u>, 9 October 1867.
[22] <u>Aurora As It Is</u>, 118.
[23] Susan Palmer, 33.
[24] "Aurora's Growth," Aurora Beacon-News, 5 September 1937, sec. 3, p. 5.

Chapter 2, Strangers Among Strangers

[25] U.S. Bureau of the Census, Seventh U.S. Census of Population, 1850, Micro copy 432 112, roll 2, volume 2, Kane County Illinois.
[26] Aurora Guardian, Wednesday, 23 February 1853.
[27] Seventh U.S. Census of Population, 1850.
[28] Carter G. Woodson, A Century of Negro Migration (Washington, D. C.: The Association for the Study of Negro Life and History, 1918), 115.
[29] Newton Bateman, Historical Encyclopedia of Illinois and History of Kane County, Illustrated (Chicago: Munsell Publishing Co., 1904), 483.
[30] Stephen Middleton, The Black Laws in the Old Northwest: A Documentary History (Westport, CT: Greenwood Press, 1993), 271-272.
[31] Ibid., 272.
[32] Solon Justice Buck, Illinois in 1818, 2nd ed. (Chicago: A. C. McClurg & Co., 1918), 94.
[33] Middleton, quoting from the Constitution of Illinois, Article 6, 1818, 278.
[34] Ibid., 273
[35] Bateman, 483.
[36] Middleton, 273.
[37] John C. W. Bailey, Kane County Directory for 1859-60 (Chicago: Press and Tribune Steam Book and Job Print, 1859), 52.
[38] U. S. Bureau of the Census, Eighth Census of the United States, 1860, Micro copy 653 191, roll 3, volume 3, Kane County, Illinois.
[39] Andy Lee, "Privileges and Views of Andy Lee, A. C. of A. D.," Aurora Beacon, 3 January 1867.
[40] "Freedmen's Aid Society," Aurora Beacon, Thursday, 2 March 1865.
[41] Gordon, 105.
[42] The Aurora City and Business Directory for 1870-71 (Chicago: C.J. Burroughs, Book Printer, 1870), 22.
[43] Henderson H. Donald, The Negro Migration of 1916-1918 (Washington, D.C.: The Association for the Study of Negro Life and History, 1921), 68.
[44] Gordon, 7.
[45] Timothy Samuelson (1986). Reading excerpted from "Black Metropolis Thematic Nomination" (Cook County, Illinois) National Register of Historic Places Registration Form, Washington, D.C.: U.S. Department of the Interior, National Park Service. Retrieved 25 March 2005 from the National Park Service Web site: http://www.cr.nps.gov/nr/twkp/wwwlps/lessons/53black/53factsr.htm.
[46] Woodson, 171-72.
[47] Robert Bruce Grant, "The Negro Comes to the City: A Documentary History From the Great Migration to the Great Depression" (Ph.D. diss., Columbia University, 1976), 342.
[48] David M. Katzman, "Black Migration." Full text Copyright Houghton Mifflin Co., 1991. Retrieved 25 March 2005, from the Answers.com web site: http://www.answers.com/topic/black-migration.
[49] Woodson, 172-73.

Chapter 3, Liberal Ideals, Racial Biases

[50] Derry, In the Beginning, 25-26.
[51] Semi-Centennial Celebration of the First Congregational Church, of Aurora, Ill., June 10th and 11th, 1888: To Which is Appended the Manual of the Church, and Complete List of Members (Aurora, IL: Press of Bunnell & Ward, 1888), 25.
[52] Ibid., 59.
[53] Ibid., 27.
[54] "Last Rites for Pioneer Woman Resident Held," Aurora Beacon-News, 10 September 1928; Julia Pfrangle to "Lutz" White, reproduced in "Now and Then," Aurora Beacon-News, 21 February 1932; "Messenger Tells Historical Tale: Fugitive Slaves in Aurora," Aurora Beacon-News, 19 March 1966.
[55] Aurora Guardian, Wednesday, 23 February 1853.
[56] Ibid.
[57] "Lutz" White, "Now and Then," Aurora Beacon-News, 1 May 1927.
[58] Aurora Beacon, Friday, 31 August 1855.
[59] Aurora Beacon, Thursday, 15 August 1850.
[60] "Lutz" White, "Now and Then," Aurora Beacon-News, 1 May 1927 (quoting the Aurora Guardian of 7 December 1854).
[61] "Lutz White, "Now and Then," Aurora Beacon-News, 1 May 1927.
[62] Ibid.
[63] Ibid.
[64] "Lutz" White, "Now and Then," Aurora Beacon-News, 1 May 1927 (quoting from a Chicago Tribune report of the convention proceedings); "Lutz" White, "Now and Then," Aurora Beacon-News, 24 April 1927 (quoting a passage from Stephen A. Douglas' debate with Abraham Lincoln at Quincy, IL).
[65] "Lutz" White, "Now and Then," Aurora Beacon-News, 24 April 1927.
[66] Rev. J. G. Bartholomew, "Slavery and the Higher Law: A Sermon, Suggested by the Execution of John Brown; and Delivered in Empire Hall, Aurora, Ill., On Sunday, Dec. 4th, 1859" (Aurora, IL: Frank E. Reynolds, 1859), 6.
[67] Ibid., 15.
[68] Ibid., 21.
[69] Ibid., 12-14.
[70] Ibid., 16.
[71] Grant, 12.
[72] "Aurora's Growth," Aurora Beacon-News, Centennial Edition, 5 September 1937, sec. 3, p. 5.
[73] Grant, 20.
[74] "Great Northwestern Fair for Benefit of the N. W. Freedmen's Aid Commission," Aurora Beacon, Thursday, 24 November 1864.
[75] Aurora Beacon, Thursday, 24 November 1864.
[76] Ibid.
[77] Aurora Beacon, Thursday, 24 November 1864.
[78] "Freedmen's Aid Society," Aurora Beacon, Thursday, 2 March 1865.
[79] Ibid.
[80] Ibid.
[81] "Report of the Northwestern Freedmen's Aid Commission," Aurora Beacon, 27 April 1865.
[82] Ibid.

[83] "Freedmen's Aid Meeting," <u>Aurora Beacon</u>, 21 November 1867.
[84] Ibid.
[85] "Negro Suffrage is a Necessity," <u>Aurora Beacon</u>, 8 June 1865.
[86] "The Word 'White,'" <u>Aurora Beacon</u>, 31 January 1867.
[87] "The Fifteenth Amendment," <u>Aurora Beacon</u>, Thursday, 16 February 1870.
[88] <u>Aurora Beacon</u>, 18 May 1870.

Chapter 4, Unpleasant Glory
This title comes from Chapter 38 of <u>The Adventures of Huckleberry Finn</u>, by Samuel Clemens

[89] Darren Ryhm, <u>The NAACP</u>, (Philadelphia: Chelsea House Publishers, 2002), 11-12.
[90] Robert A. Gibson (1978), "Booker T. Washington and W. E. B. DuBois: The Problem of Negro Leadership," retrieved 17 March, 2005, from Yale University Web site: http://www.cis.yale.edu/ynhti/curriculum/units/1978/2/78.02.02.x.html
[91] Ibid.
[92] Grant, 20.
[93] Isaiah Carter, interview by Mike Sarna, tape recording, 9 April 1988, Aurora Historical Society, Aurora, IL.
[94] <u>Aurora Beacon</u>, 25 February 1864.
[95] <u>Aurora Beacon</u>, 3 March 1864.
[96] <u>Aurora Beacon</u>, 10 March 1864.
[97] Donald, 63 and 71.
[98] Grant, 17.
[99] Ibid., 132.
[100] Ibid., 17.
[101] Ibid., 159.
[102] Ibid., 159.
[103] Isaiah Carter, interviewed 9 April 1988.
[104] Ibid.
[105] Ibid.
[106] Ibid.
[107] "Lutz" White, "Now and Then," <u>Aurora Beacon-News</u>, 25 March 1934.
[108] Letter to "Lutz" White from "Y.M.S.C.," reprinted in "Now and Then," <u>Aurora Beacon-News</u>, 4 July 1926.
[109] "Lutz" White, "Now and Then," <u>Aurora Beacon-News</u>, 25 March 1934.
[110] "History of Our Church," <u>The 100th Anniversary of St. John A.M.E. Church Souvenir Program</u>, 1962.
[111] Congregational Directory, Main Baptist Church, 1985.
[112] "The Poor of Aurora," <u>Aurora Beacon</u>, 1 January 1873.
[113] Grant, 319.
[114] <u>Aurora Beacon</u>, 8 March 1876.
[115] <u>Aurora As It Is</u>, 118.
[116] <u>Aurora Beacon</u>, 9 July 1873.
[117] <u>Aurora Beacon</u>, 21 February 1883.
[118] <u>Aurora Beacon</u>, 19 October 1872.
[119] Arthur Diamond, <u>Prince Hall, Social Reformer</u> (New York: Chelsea House Publishers, 1992), 55.
[120] <u>Aurora Beacon</u>, 1 January 1873.

121 Diamond, 59.
122 James McNeil, phone interview with author, 17 July 1999.
123 Ibid.
124 Aurora Beacon, 30 April 1908.
125 Gordon, 53.
126 Palmer, 25.
127 Henrietta Reynolds to "Lutz" White, reprinted in "Now and Then," Aurora Beacon-News, 2 August 1931.
128 Lloyd Ochsenschalger to "Lutz" White, reprinted in "Now and Then," Aurora Beacon-News, 18 March 1934.
129 Ibid.
130 Isaiah Carter, interviewed 9 April 1988.
131 Paid advertisement, Aurora Beacon, 7 June 1873.
132 "Lutz" White, "Now and Then," Aurora Beacon-News, 13 March 1927.
133 "Lutz" White, "Now and Then," Aurora Beacon-News, 5 April 1925.
134 Aurora Beacon, 8 July 1876.
135 Text of speech given by Rev. William Bartlett, reprinted in Aurora Beacon, 8 July 1876.
136 Aurora Beacon, 8 July 1876.
137 Aurora Beacon, 12 January 1876; Aurora Beacon, 8 March 1876.
138 James DeVries, Race and Kinship in a Midwestern Town: The Black Experience in Monroe, Michigan, 1900-1915 (Chicago: University of Illinois Press, 1984), 108.
139 Aurora Beacon, 15 March 1890.
140 Jeanne Boger Jones, telephone interview with author, 7 March 2005.
141 Henry Boger, in France, to his mother in Aurora, IL, 1 September 1918, from the collection of Jeanne Boger Jones.
142 Henry Boger, in France, to his brothers and sister in Aurora, IL, 16 October 1918, from the collection of Jeanne Boger Jones.
143 Obituary for Calvin T. Boger, The Aurora Daily Beacon-News, 6 January 1925.
144 "Lutz" White, "Now and Then," The Aurora Daily Beacon-News, 22 May 1932.
145 Abner Hard, M.D., History of the Eighth Cavalry Regiment Illinois Volunteers, During the Great Rebellion (Aurora, IL: n.p., 1868); E. G. Bennett and William H. Haigh, History of the Thirty-sixth Regiment Illinois Volunteers, During the War of the Rebellion (Aurora, IL: Knickerbocker and Hodder, Printers and Binders, 1876).
146 Jeanne Boger Jones, telephone interview with author, 7 March 2005.
147 Palmer, 193-95.
148 Woodson, 172.
149 Andy Lee, "Privileges and Views of Andy Lee, A. C. of A. D.," Aurora Beacon, 3 January 1867.

SOURCES CONSULTED

"Abstract of the Second Annual Report of the Board of Directors of theNorthwestern
 Freedmen's Aid Commission, presented at the
 Anniversary Meeting held in Bryan Hall, Chicago, on Thursday
 Evening, April 13th, 1865." <u>Aurora Beacon</u>. 27 April 1865.

Alft, E. G. <u>Elgin's Black Heritage</u>. Elgin, IL: City of Elgin, 1996.

<u>Atlas of Kane County, Illinois: Drawn and Compiled From Personal
 Observations, Actual Surveys and County Records</u>. Chicago: D. W.
 Ensign & Co., 1892.

<u>Aurora As It Is: The First Annual Gazetteer and City Directory for Aurora,
 Illinois</u>. Aurora, IL: Knickerbocker and Hodder, 1868.

<u>Aurora Beacon</u>. 15 August 1850.

---.   31 August 1855.

---.   25 February 1864.

---.   3 March 1864.

---.   10 March 1864.

---.   24 November 1864.

---.   9 October 1867.

---.   18 May 1870.

---.   19 October 1872.

---.   1 January 1873.

---.   7 June 1873.

---.   9 July 1873.

---.   12 January 1876.

---.   8 March 1876.

Aurora Beacon. 8 July 1876.

---. 21 February 1883.

---. 15 March 1890.

---. 30 April 1908.

Aurora City and Business Directory for 1870-71. Chicago: C. J. Burroughs, Book Printer, 1870.

Aurora Guardian. Wednesday, 23 February 1853.

"Aurora Government and Institutions: a class project conducted in civics under the supervision of T.L. Carlson." Aurora, IL: East Aurora High School, 1941.

"Aurora's Growth." Aurora Beacon-News. 5 September 1937, sec. 3 p. 5.

Aurora, Illinois, Illustrated. Aurora, IL: J.H. Hodder, 1890.

Aurora Preservation Commission. Historic Aurora, Near Eastside Walking Tour. Aurora, IL: 1982.

---. Historic Aurora, Near Northwest Walking Tour. Aurora, IL: 1982.

---. Time Line of the City of Aurora, 1800 - 1956.

"Aurora Served by 46 Mayors Since the First, B. F. Hall, Took Office in 1857." Aurora Beacon-News. 5 September 1937, sec. 3, p. 4.

Bailey, John C. W. Kane County Directory for 1859-60. Chicago: Press and Tribune Steam Book and Job Print, 1859.

Barclay, Robert, ed. "Now and Then." Aurora Daily Beacon-News. 1962-1976.

Battle, Charles S. Centennial Biographical and Historical Record of Aurora for One Hundred Years 1834-1937 and the Chicago, Burlington & Quincy Railroad for Eighty-six Years 1850-1937. Aurora, IL: Aurora Bicentennial Commission, 1937.

Bennett, E. G., and William H. Haigh. <u>History of the Thirty-Sixth Regiment Illinois Volunteers, During the War of the Rebellion</u>. Aurora, IL: Knickerbocker and Hodder, Printers and binders, 1876.

Boger, Henry, France, to mother, Aurora, IL, 1 September 1918. Private collection of Jeanne Boger Jones, Aurora, IL.

---. France, to brothers and sister, Aurora, IL. 16 October 1918. Private collection of Jeanne Boger Jones, Aurora, IL.

Buck, Solon Justus. <u>Illinois in 1818</u>, 2nd ed. Chicago: A.C. McClurg and Company, 1918.

Burton, Charles Pierce, ed. "Now and Then." <u>Aurora Daily Beacon-News</u>, 1935-1947.

Burton, Charles Pierce. <u>Aurora from Covered Wagon to Stream-Lined Zephyr</u>. Aurora, IL: Aurora Centennial Association, 1937.

Carter, Isaiah. Interview by Michael Sarna, 9 April 1988. Tape recording. Aurora Historical Society, Aurora, IL.

Chang, Dayna, Felicia Maianu and Jim Tinnell. "Community, Signs and Symbols: An Ethnography." Wheaton, IL: Wheaton College, 1994

Congregational Directory, Main Baptist Church, 1985.

Deering, Roberta, and Joseph McElroy. <u>Historic Structures of Stolp Island</u>. Aurora Preservation Commission, 1985.

Derry, Vernon. <u>Aurora. . .In the Beginning</u>. Aurora, IL: Kelmscott Press, 1953.

---. <u>Aurora in the Gay '90s 1892-1910</u>. Aurora, IL: Strathmore, 1967.

---. <u>The Aurora Story</u>. Aurora, IL: Aurora Bicentennial Commission, 1976.

---. <u>Thrift Corner Yarns</u>. Aurora, IL: Aurora Savings and Loan, 1967.

DeVries, James E. <u>Race and Kinship in a Midwestern Town: The Black Experience In Monroe, Michigan, 1900-1915</u>. Chicago: University of Illinois Press, 1984.

Diamond, Arthur. <u>Prince Hall, Social Reformer</u>. New York: Chelsea House Publishers, 1992.

Donald, Henderson H. The Negro Migration of 1916-1918. Washington, D. C.:
The Association for the Study of Negro Life and History, 1921.

Durant, Pliney A. Biographical and Historical Record of Kane County, Illinois.
Chicago: Beers, Legget, 1888.

Faye, Stanley, ed. "Now and Then." Aurora Daily Beacon-News. 1947-1948.

"The Fifteenth Amendment." Aurora Beacon. 16 February 1870.

"Freedmen's Aid Society." Aurora Beacon. 2 March 1865.

Gibson, Robert A. (1978) "Booker T. Washington and W.E.B. DuBois: The
Problem of Negro Leadership." Retrieved 17 March, 2005, from the Yale
University Web site:
http://www.cis.yale.edu/ynhti/curriculum/units/1978/2/78.02.02.x.html

Gordon, Milton M. Assimilation in American Life: The Role of Race, Religion
and National Origins. New York: Oxford University Press, 1964.

Grant, Robert Bruce. The Negro Comes to the City: A Documentary History
From the Great Migration to the Great Depression. Ph.D. dissertation,
Columbia University, 1976.

"Great Northwestern Fair for Benefit of the N. W. Freedmen's Aid
Commission." Aurora Beacon. 24 November 1864.

Hard, Abner, M.D. History of the Eighth Cavalry Regiment Illinois
Volunteers, During the Great Rebellion. Aurora, IL: n.p., 1868.

Hattwick, Richard E. The Aurora Metal Company. Macomb, IL: Western
Illinois University Center for Business and Economic Research, 1976.

---.   Barber-Greene. Macomb, IL: Western Illinois University Center for Business
and Economic Research, 1976.

Hattwick, Richard E. A Tale of Three Sheet Metal Fabricators: All Steel, Equipto and
Lyon Metal. Macomb, IL: Western Illinois University Center for Business and
Economic Research, 1976.

"History of Our Church." The 100th Anniversary of St. John A. M. E. Church
Souvenir Program, n.p. 1962.

Holland's Triennial City Directory of Aurora, Illinois for the Years 1890-93, In Three Parts, Containing Respectively Historical, Editorial and Business Departments. Chicago: Holland Publishing Company, 1890.

Jones, Jeanne Boger. Telephone interview conducted by author, 7 March 2005.

Joslyn, L.L.M., and Frank W. Joslyn. History of Kane County, Illinois. Chicago: Pioneer Publishing, 1908.

Katzman, David M. "Black Migration." Full text Copyright Houghton Mifflin Co., 1991. Retrieved 25 March, 2005, from the Answers.com web site: http://www.answers.com/topic/black-migration.

Know Your Town. Aurora, IL: League of Women Voters, 1959.

---. Aurora, IL: League of Women Voters, 1964.

---. Aurora, IL: League of Women Voters, 1985.

McNeil, James. Telephone interview conducted by author, 18 July 1999.

M'Dole, A. G., comp. The Charter and Ordinances of the City of Aurora (To June 1, 1863, Inclusive), Together With the Acts of the General Assembly Relating to the City, and Other Miscellaneous Acts. Aurora, IL: Bangs and Knickerbocker, 1863.

"Messenger Tells Historical Tale: Fugitive Slaves in Aurora." Aurora Beacon-News, 19 March 1966.

Middleton, Stephen. The Black Laws In the Old Northwest: A Documentary History. Westport, CT: Greenwood Press, 1993.

Moore, John H., ed. Aurora, 1964. Aurora, IL: Aurora College, 1964.

Moore, John H. A Study of Metropolitan Fringe. Aurora, IL: Aurora College, 1961

Morey, Russell and William Scott. Garbe Iron Works, Inc. Macomb, IL: Western Illinois University Center for Business and Economic Research, 1976.

"Negro Suffrage is a Necessity." Aurora Beacon. 8 June 1865.

"Obituary for Calvin T. Boger." Aurora Beacon-News. 16 January 1925.

O'Brien, Frances Jean. "A Study of Aurora Schools, 1835-1935." Thesis, Northern Illinois University, 1990.

Palmer, Susan L. Building Ethnic Communities in a Small City: Romanians and Mexicans in Aurora, Illinois, 1900-1940. Ph.D. dissertation, Northern Illinois University, 1986.

Plum, Jennie L. Aurora, Illinois, 1905. Aurora, IL: 1905.

"The Poor of Aurora." Aurora Beacon. 1 January 1873.

Pritchard, E. R. Illinois of Today and its Progressive Cities. Chicago: 1897.

Ryhm, Darren. The NAACP. Philadelphia: Chelsea House Publishers, 2002.

Samuelson, Timothy (1986). Reading excerpted from "Black Metropolis Thematic Nomination" (Cook County, Illinois) National Register of Historic Places Registration Form, Washington, D.C.: U.S. Department of the Interior, National Park Service. Retrieved 25 March 2005 from the National Park Service Web site: http://www.cr.nps.gov/nr/twkp/wwwlps/lessons/53black/53factsr.htm.

Semi-Centennial Celebration of the First Congregational Church, of Aurora, Ill., June 10th and 11th, 1888: To Which is Appended the Manual of the Church, And Complete List of Members. Aurora, IL: Press of Bunnell & Ward, 1888.

U.S. Bureau of the Census. A Compendium of the Ninth Census, June 1, 1870. Washington, D.C.: Government Printing Office, 1872.

---. Sixth Census of the United States, 1840. Micro copy No. 704 62, roll 1, volume 1, Kane County, Illinois.

---. Seventh U.S. Census of Population, 1850. Micro copy No. 432 112, roll 2, volume 2, Kane County, Illinois.

---. Eighth Census of the United States, 1860. Micro copy No. 653 191, roll 3, volume 3, Kane County, Illinois.

---. Ninth Census of the United States, 1870. Micro copy No. 593 236, roll 4, volume 4, Aurora, Kane County, Illinois.

---. Tenth Census of the United States, 1880. Micro copy No. T9 217, roll 6, volume 6, Aurora, Kane County, Illinois.

U.S. Bureau of the Census. Tenth Census of the United States, 1880. Micro copy No. T 9 218, roll 7, volume 7, Aurora, Kane County, Illinois.

---. Twelfth Census of the United States, 1900. Micro copy No. T 623 310, volume 8, Enumeration Districts 60 – 75.

---. Twelfth Census of the United States, 1900. Micro copy No. T 623 311, volume 9, Enumeration Districts 75 – 92.

---. Twelfth Census of the United States, 1900. Micro copy No. T 623 312, volume 10, Enumeration Districts 93 – 116 – 166.

---. Thirteenth Census of the United States, 1910. Micro Copy No. T 624, roll 296, volume 12, Aurora City.

---. Thirteenth Census of the United States, 1910. Micro Copy No. T 624, roll 295, volume 14, Aurora Township.

---. Fourteenth Census of the United States, 1920. Micro Copy No. T 625 373, volume 156, Enumeration Districts 32-45.

---. Fourteenth Census of the United States, 1920. Micro Copy No. T 625 374, v. 157 and 158, Enumeration Districts 46-75, 96-111.

---. Fourteenth Census of the United States, 1920. Micro Copy No. T 625 375, volume 159, Enumeration Districts 76- 95.

White, "Lutz," ed. "Now and Then." Aurora Daily Beacon-News. 1925-1935.

Wells Engineering Company. Plat Book of Aurora, Kane County, Illinois (being copies of the plats as recorded for record in the recorder's office of Kane County, Illinois). Rockford, IL: The Thrift Press.

Woodson, Carter G. A Century of Negro Migration. Washington, D. C.: The Association for the Study of Negro Life and History, 1918.

"The Word White." Aurora Beacon. 31 January 1867.

INDEX

A

African American History Museum and Black Veterans Archive · 9
African Americans
    "Contraband of war" · 40, 96
    Churches as gathering places · 106, 109
    Education of · 46–48, 49–51, 56, 59
    Employment of · 45–46, 48–49, 57, 62–63
    Home ownership · 42–43, 48, 57, 63
    Housing · *114*
    Migration to Aurora · 42–43, 48, 51, 56, 59–61
    Population by decade · 41
    Population, by place of birth · 44
    Response to racism · 90–94, 99–104, 115, 117–21, 123, 125–29, 135–36
    Settlement patterns · 43–45, 48, 51–53, 56–57, 61–62, 112–15
    Social organizations · 104, 106–12
Artis, Annie · 49, 51
Atlanta Compromise, The · 92
Attucks, Crispus · 120
Aurora
    City charter · 22–24
    City map, 1860 · *23*
    City map, 1868 · *39*
    City map, 1892 · *52*
    East-West rivalry · 22–24, 26–27, 117
    First African American Residents · 30
    Founding · 17–20
    Immigration to · 25, 26–27, 42–43, 48, 51, 56, 59–61, 94, 133
    Incorporated · 20
    Named · 20
    Neighborhoods · 26–27, 43–45, 48, 51–53, 56, 61, 112–15
    Plat map, 1836 · *21*
    School system · 48, 49–51, 56, 59, 85–87
    Total population by decade · 29
Aurora Beacon-News · 28, 83
    Abolitionist views · 68, 79–80
    Coverage of African Americans · 78, 106, 107–08, 111, 117, 123
    Now & Then column · 13, 102–03, 112–15, 129–33
    Editorials on voting rights · 40, 83–84
    Editorial on education · 84–85
    Aurora Brewing Company · 26
    Aurora Guardian
    Abolitionist views · 68–70
    Support for Underground Railroad · 70, 71
Aurora Historical Society · 8, 15
    Mission Statement · 137
Aurora Volksfreund · 28

B

Barbers · 45, *47*, 49, 53, 102–4
Barclay, Robert · 13
Barnett, Rev. · 104
"Barracks, The" · 112, *113*
Bartholomew, Rev. J.G. · 81
    Anti-slavery sermon · 74–77
Bartlett, Rev. William A. · 120
Beacon · See <u>Aurora Beacon-News</u>
Bell, Samuel · 57
Blackface · 121, *124*
Boger, Calvin · 108, 110, *128*, 129–33, 136
    Obituary · 129
Boger, Henry · 125–27, *127*, 136
    Letters home · 125, 126
Boll weevil · 60
Bora, Joseph · 30
Brady School · 115, *116*
"Brer Rabbit" · 92
Broadway, looking north · *47*
Brown, John · 74
Brown's Coal · *89*
Burton, Charles Pierce · 13
Buttons, Rev. · 104

C

Carter, Ben, and family · *95*
Carter, "Ike" · See Carter, Isaiah
Carter, Isaiah · 94, *100*, 115, 136
    Interview with · 99–102
Cattlet, Catherine · 94
Chicago, Illinois · 24, 25
    African American population · 61
    Attracting immigrants · 56, 59, 61, 70, 94, 132–33
    Founded · 32
Chicago and Aurora Smelting and Refining Company · 57
Chicago, Burlington & Quincy Railroad · 24–26, 28, 38
<u>Chicago Defender</u> · 60–61
Civil War · 38, 41, 42, 74, 129–31
Clark, George Rogers · 32

Coleman, Edmund · 45, 108, 110
Collins, John · 108

D

Dane, Nathan · 32
DeCoursey, Eva · 49
DeCoursey, Milton · 49, 108, 110
    Barbershop · *47*
Defender · See Chicago Defender
Demery, David · 36–38, 78
Demery, Julia · 36–38
Demery, Sarah · 38
Democratic Party · 64, 65, 68, 71, 72, 77
Discrimination
    By employers · 96–98
    By unions · 98–102
Douglas, Stephen A. · 71–72
Douglass, Frederick · 71–72
DuBois, W.E.B. · 93, 136
Dubrock's Quartet · *88*
DuSable, Jean Baptiste Pointe · 31
Dyer, Charles · 57

E

Eberly, Gilbert · *55*
Emancipation Celebration · 107–8
Emancipation Proclamation · 13, 40, 43, 79

F

Faye, Stanley · 13
Fifteenth Amendment · 83–84
Fillmore, Millard · 67
First Congregational Church · 65, *66*
    Abolitionism · 65
    Called "Union Depot" · 67, 70
First Presbyterian Church · 65, *66*
Fox River · 17, 22
    Stolp Island · 16
"Free Soil" Democrats · 65, 71, 77
Freedmen's Aid Society · 81–82
Freemasonry
    Social importance · 108–10

French and Indian War · *See* Seven Years War
Fugitive Slave Law · 35, 64, 67, 71, 73, 76, 77

G

Geneva, Illinois · 72
Giddings, Franklin · 111
Gigger, Emma · 53
Gillman, George · 36–38, 78
Gillman, Mary · 36–38
Gordon, Milton · 27, 45, 111
Grant, Robert Bruce · 60, 62
Great Migration · 59–61
Guardian · See Aurora Guardian

H

Hall, John · 108
Hallock, Rev. J.A. · 65
Hard, Dr. Abner · 130
Harlem Renaissance · 14
Hartford, Illinois · 20
Hattery, Captain · 130
Hercules Iron Works · 26
Holland, Billy · ***91***

I

Idle Hour Club · 118, ***119***
Illinois
    Black Laws · 34
    Black Laws rescinded · 41
    Granted Statehood · 34
    Slavery in · 32–35
    Slavery introduced · 32
Indentured Service · 31, 33–34
Independence Day, 1876
    Calathumpian Parade · 121
    Parade · 120
Independence Day, 1913
    Parade entry · ***122***
Isham, W.J. · 108

J

Jackson, Carrie · 2, *50*, 137
Jackson, J. · 108
Jackson, Michigan · 73
Jackson, Minnie · 57
Jefferson, Thomas · 32
"Jim Crow" laws · 59
Jones, Jeanne Boger · 131
Jungels, "Pug" · *91*

K

Kansas-Nebraska Act · 65, 71, 73, 77
Keystone Lodge · 108–10
Knights of Pythias · 110
Ku Klux Klan · 59–60

L

Labor Day, 1903 · *132*
Ladies' Christian Union, The · 106
Lake, Theodore · *19*, 20
Lake, Zaphna · 17
LaMar, Pete · 121
Landry, Octave · 112
Lee, Andy · 13, 40–41, 136
Lincoln, Abraham · 43
Long, Martin · 121
Lucas, Alfred · 53

M

Main Street, corner of LaSalle and · *102*
Main Street Baptist Church · 12, *105*
    Founding · 104
Manuel, Barton
    Barbershop · 47
Mason, Ben · 118–20, 135
McCarty Mills, Illinois · 20
McCarty, Joseph · 17
McCarty, Samuel · 17, *18*, 20, 24
McNeil, James · 110
Meadows, James · 112, 117–18, *119*, 121, 135

Sons of · 115
Minstrel Shows · 123, 124
Mississippi River
    Floods · 60
Missouri Compromise · 64, 65
Mix and Miller's Bank · 110
Morton, John · *54*
Morton, Theodore · *55*
Muse, Marie · 57

N

National Association for the Advancement of Colored People · 14, 136
New York Street School · *86*
North Western Freedmen's Aid Commission · 42, 79–81, 82
Northwest Ordinance · 32–33, 35

O

Ochsenschlager, Lloyd · 112, 115

P

Palmer, Susan · 26, 112, 132, 133
Park Place Baptist Church · 104
Parker, William · 36
Parks, Benjamin Franklin · 72
Parsons, Rev. W.L. · 65
Peck, Sheldon · 68
Pug's Colts · *91*

Q

Quincy, Illinois · 42, 85

R

Race
    19th century theories on · 77
    Diversity in Aurora · 26–27
Rathbone, Sard & Company · 26, 57
Reconstruction · 92
Republican Party · 65, 76, 83, 84, 94, 129, 131

Congressional Convention in Aurora, 1854 · 72–74
Ripon, Wisconsin · 73

S

Sacred Heart Roman Catholic Church · 27
Seven Years War · 32
"Signifying Monkey" · 92, 120
Smith, John · 102, 104
St. John's African Methodist Episcopal Church · 12
    Founding · 104
Stewart, James · 108
Stolp Island · *16*, *37*
Stowe, Harriet Beecher · 76

T

Talented Tenth, The · 93, 136
Thomasson, Clark · 108
Triggs, Matilda · 118, 123
    House · *37*
Turkey Club · *54*
Tuskegee Institute · 92

U

Uncle Tom's Cabin · 76
Underground Railroad · 9, 35, 65, 67, 68, 70, 78
Universalist Church · *66*, 74
Urban League · 14

V

Volksfreund · See Aurora Volksfreund

W

Wagner family portrait · *69*
Wagner, John J. · 67
Wagner, Laura · 67
Wagner, Maria · 67
Wallace, Frances · 57
Washington, Booker T. · 92, 136

Webb, Mose · 102, 104, 108, 110
　　Candy Shop · *103*
Webster, Daniel · 71
West Aurora, Illinois
　　Incorporated · 22
　　Named · 20
West Aurora High School · 124
Wheaton, Charles · 67
Whig Party · 64–65, 68, 70, 71, 72
White, Lewis · 13, 70, 118, 129–132
White, "Lutz" · *See* White, Lewis
Wilcox Manufacturing Company · 57
Woodson, Carter G. · 62, 133
Woolson, F.W.
　　Barbershop · *55*
World War I · 60, 62, 125–29